Introduction to the Study of the *Classic of Change* (*I-hsüeh ch'i-meng*)

by Chu Hsi

Translated by
Joseph A. Adler
Kenyon College

*Bilingual Texts in
Chinese History, Philosophy and Religion*
John Chaffee, Executive Editor

Number 1

Global Scholarly Publications

Copyright © 2002 by Global Scholarly Publications

All rights reserved. No portion of this publication may be duplicated in any way without the expressed written consent of the publisher, except in the form of brief excerpts or quotations for review purposes.

Library of Congress Cataloging-in-Publication Data

Chu Hsi, *Introduction to the Study of the Classic of Change*
Translated by Joseph A. Adler

ISBN 1-59267-334-1

Published by Global Scholarly Publications
Brigham Young University, Provo, Utah
Distributed by Global Scholarly Publications
220 Madison Avenue
New York, New York 10016
Phone: (212) 679-6410   Fax: (212) 679-6424
E-mail: books@gsp-online.org

Sponsored by:

Global Scholarly Publications
A subsidiary of
The Foundation for Interreligious Diplomacy

Executive Committee:
Parviz Morewedge: the Director of GSP (*Rutgers University, New Brunswick*), Charles Randall Paul (*President, Foundation for Interreligious Diplomacy [FID], Utah*), Daniel C. Peterson (*Brigham Young University, Director of Institute for the Study and Preservation of Ancient Religious Texts*), Chun-Fang Yu (*Rutgers University, New Brunswick*) and Gerald Snow (*the Legal Counsel of GSP*).

Institute for the Study and Preservation of Ancient Religious Texts
Brigham Young University, Provo, Utah

and

Association of Chinese Philosophers in America

Consortium for Bilingual Texts in Chinese History, Philosophy and Religion

Editorial Board:

John Chaffee (*Binghamton University*), Executive Editor
John Berthrong (*Boston University*)
Zu-yan Chen (*Binghamton University*)
Ron Guey Chu (*Gettysburg College*)
David Honey (*Brigham Young University*)
Yong Huang (*Kutzdown University*)
Lisa Raphals (*University of California at Riverside*)
Chun-fang Yu (*Rutgers University*)

CONTENTS

Introduction	i
Appendix: The Sixty-Four Hexagrams	xii
Preface	1
I. The Original "Chart" and "Text"	3
II. Original Drawing of the Trigrams	15
III. Explaining the Milfoil Stalks	33
IV. Examining the Prognostications of the Changes	48
Notes	54

Figures 1-2	following page 2
Figures 3-12	following page 32
Figures 13-18	following page 47
Figures 19.1-19.21	following page 53

Introduction[1]

The *I-hsüeh ch'i-meng* (Introduction to the Study of the *Classic of Change*), by Chu Hsi (1130-1200), is a short text that lies at the intersection of two monumental products and shapers of the Chinese intellectual tradition. The *I Ching* (*Classic of Change*), known more commonly in Chinese literature as the *Chou I* (*Changes of Chou*), was originally a divination manual used by the aristocracy of the Chou dynasty (11th-3rd c. BCE) to determine the advisability and potential outcomes of specific courses of action they were contemplating. The core of the text is sixty-four six-line diagrams (*kua*) or hexagrams, each composed of a pair of three-line diagrams, or trigrams. Each line can be either solid, symbolizing *yang* (light, active, rising, expanding), or broken, symbolizing *yin* (dark, passive, sinking, contracting).[2] Over the course of centuries it acquired various layers of commentary, and became widely known as a compendium of the most profound insights into the nature and patterns of the Way (*tao*). It is one of the "Five Classics" associated with Confucius (551-479 BCE), who is traditionally credited with having written the appendices (the "Ten Wings") that became part of the text itself -- although scholars since the eleventh century have acknowledged that this is very unlikely.[3]

As a Confucian text, the *I Ching* is considered to be a guide to moral behavior. According to this way of thinking, when the proper course of action is unclear one can use the text as an oracle to get a "reading," so to speak, of the *tao* at that moment in time, which is determined by the set of circumstances in which one is acting. Since circumstances are constantly changing, the reading one derives from the *I Ching* includes a directional component, or tendency, that can be extrapolated to a potential future outcome. But that outcome

Introduction

is contingent upon one's ability to interpret the reading correctly and, most importantly, to act in harmony with the flow of events. Thus, from a Confucian perspective, the text is best used as an aid to moral self-cultivation, since it helps one to understand the morally appropriate response to circumstances when otherwise one might be at a loss what to do.

The other pillar of the Chinese intellectual-religious tradition represented by the *I-hsüeh ch'i-meng* is its author, Chu Hsi, who was probably the most influential Chinese thinker after Confucius. Chu Hsi was the architect of what became the orthodox version of "Neo-Confucianism" – the revival of Confucianism that began in the eleventh century, incorporating elements of Taoism and Buddhism into a synthesis based on the Mencian strand of Confucian thought.[4] Chu Hsi wove together some of the new Confucian theories that had arisen in the eleventh century into a creative synthesis that became the dominant school of Chinese religious philosophy until the twentieth century.[5] His interpretations of the Confucian tradition became the officially sanctioned ideology that had to be mastered by literati who took the civil service examinations to qualify for government service. This influence on the Chinese intellectual world lasted from 1313 to 1905, and extended to Japan and Korea as well.

The *I-hsüeh ch'i-meng* was the second of two books Chu Hsi wrote on the *I Ching*. The first was a commentary, entitled *Chou-i pen-i* (Original Meaning of the *Classic of Change*), which was completed in 1177 and revised sometime after 1186.[6] The meaning of the title is significant, for by the Sung dynasty (960-1279 CE) the *I Ching* had acquired not only the "Ten Wings" but also hundreds of commentaries by later scholars. Chu's commentary was an attempt to move beyond the later accretions of interpretation embodied in the Ten Wings and the later commentaries, and to penetrate to the original meanings intended by the sages who were thought to have been responsible for the earliest layers of the *I*. These were (1) Fu-hsi, a mythic culture hero to whom were attributed the original oracular diagrams; (2) King Wen, the first king of the Chou dynasty, who was said to have written the short texts accompanying each hexagram; and (3) his son, the Duke of Chou, who was thought to have been the author of the short texts accompanying each line of each hexagram.

Of these, Chu Hsi was especially interested in Fu-hsi ("Subduer of Animals"), who was also known as the earliest of the "Three Sovereigns" (*san sheng*) of high antiquity.[7] Besides inventing hexagram divination, Fu-hsi was credited with the invention of hunting and fishing implements, and animal sacrifice. But it was Fu-hsi's creation of the *I* that persuaded Chu Hsi to place Fu-hsi at the very beginning of the "succession of the Way" (*tao-t'ung*), the line of sages who, according to Chu, had passed down the true understanding of the Tao from antiquity to the present. This line of sages and the Tao that they had transmitted constituted a form of legitimation for Chu Hsi and his colleagues, who considered themselves to be the correct interpreters of the Confucian Way in the Sung dynasty. Earlier Confucian scholars had considered Yao and Shun (later mythic sage-kings) to be the progenitors of the Confucian Tao, but Chu Hsi pushed the beginning of the line back to Fu-hsi, in particular because of the manner in which Fu-hsi had created the *I*. This story was told in the *Hsi-tz'u* (Appended Remarks) appendix of the *I Ching*:

Introduction

> In ancient times, when Pao-hsi [=Fu-hsi] ruled the world, he looked up and contemplated the images (*hsiang*) in heaven; he looked down and contemplated the patterns (*fa*) on earth. He contemplated the markings of the birds and beasts and their adaptations to the various regions. From near at hand he abstracted images from his own body; from afar he abstracted from things. In this way he first created the Eight Trigrams,[8] to spread the power (*te*) of [his] spiritual clarity (*shen-ming*) and to classify the dispositions of the myriad things.[9]

The significance of this account for Chu is its claim that Fu-hsi created the trigrams of the *I* by intuiting the moral implications of the patterns that he observed in nature. This connection between the moral order and the natural order had always been a fundamental principle in Confucian thought. It is basically the idea that moral values are not subjective; they are inherent in the natural world. For example, Mencius had argued that morality is an innate tendency in human beings, as natural as their desires for food and sex.[10] And the *Chung-yung* (Centrality and Commonality, often translated as the Doctrine of the Mean) discusses the concept of *ch'eng* (authenticity) as both a moral and a cosmological principle.[11] Chu Hsi and his predecessors in the Ch'eng school formulated this conception in terms of the concept of *li* (order or principle), which they said is both the natural order (*t'ien-li*, or principle of Heaven) and the moral order (*tao-li*, or principle of the Way).

In Chu Hsi's view, Fu-hsi was thus the earliest sage to have seen and understood this connection – the moral implications of patterns in nature – and so his creation of the *I* was the first realization or actualization of the Confucian Tao in the world. As such, the original meaning and intention of this creative act was of utmost importance. And according to the traditional accounts (which Chu Hsi considered to be historical), the *I* that Fu-hsi created was not a book, but merely a set of hexagrams, which have since antiquity been the core of the *I Ching*. The hexagrams constituted a system of divination, in which the specific configuration of *yin* and *yang* in each hexagram could be interpreted as a dynamic picture of the situation confronting the questioner. There was no text at all until the troubled time of King Wen (the founder of the Chou dynasty in the eleventh century BCE), who felt that people were no longer capable of interpreting the hexagrams directly. While he was imprisoned by the wicked last king of the Shang dynasty (seventeenth-eleventh centuries BCE), King Wen therefore composed the texts accompanying each of the sixty-four hexagrams, to help elucidate their oracular meanings.[12] The Duke of Chou later added short texts explaining each line of each hexagram.[13] And finally, the Ten Wings or appendices became part of the text itself and were attributed to Confucius, giving them tremendous authority and appeal.[14]

For Chu Hsi, these textual layers of the *I Ching* were not the original locus of meaning. They were intended merely as clarifications of the graphic and oracular meanings of the hexagrams -- i.e. as specific configurations of *yin* and *yang* that had moral implications for human behavior. Therefore a correct interpretation of the text must make sense in that light; the *I Ching* was a book to be used, not merely studied.

However, according to Chu, scholars since the Han dynasty (206 BCE-220 CE) had lost sight of the original oracular meaning and purpose of the *I*. Two strands of commentarial tradition on the *I* had developed since the Han, both of which made this fundamental mistake. The *hsiang-shu*, or "image and number" school, focused on the graphic and

Introduction

numerological symbolism of the hexagrams and other diagrams associated with the *I*, such as the Ho-t'u (Yellow River Chart) and the Lo-shu (Lo River Text).[15] While these graphic layers were important in understanding the "natural principle" of the *I*, Chu felt that the *hsiang-shu* school in general neglected Fu-hsi's original intention by focusing on the cosmological and numerological correlations of the hexagrams instead of their oracular meanings. The major representative of this school in the Northern Sung period (960-1127) was Shao Yung (1011-1077), whom Chu Hsi quotes extensively in the first chapter of the *I-hsüeh ch'i-meng*, where he explains the Ho-t'u and Lo-shu.

The *i-li*, or "moral principle" school, on the other hand, focused on the textual layers of the *I*, deriving moral principles from the hexagram texts, the line texts, and the appendices. This school dated back at least to Wang Pi (226-249 CE), whose commentary on the *I* was tremendously influential, and in fact was recognized as "orthodox" during the T'ang dynasty (618-906). The major *i-li* commentator in the Northern Sung was Ch'eng I. Despite the fact that Chu was greatly indebted to Ch'eng for much of his philosophical system, he harshly criticized the Northern Sung master's treatment of the *I*, again for neglecting Fu-hsi's original intention in creating it. And despite Chu's belief that Confucius had written the Ten Wings (an idea that had already been refuted by Chu Hsi's time, and is not taken seriously by scholars today), he also questioned the value of these later texts as interpretive aids. The appendices, he said, reflect Confucius' own ideas about the natural/moral order. Confucius' intentions in writing them were different from those of the three earlier sages, and should therefore not be relied upon to uncover the original meaning of the basic text.

Chu Hsi's theory was that the "original intention" or purpose of the hexagrams was not philosophical but oracular: they were intended to be used to determine how to act in particular situations, not to express moral principles. Among scholars ever since Wang Pi though, the *I* had generally been used as textual support for each commentator's own ideas. This, according to Chu, was not only likely to result in specious argumentation, it was also bound to neglect the real access to the "mind of the sage" (primarily referring to Fu-hsi) that the *I* could provide. This was an existential connection, enabled by one's thorough engagement with the text, that could prove invaluable in the extremely difficult process of self-cultivation. Thus Chu repeatedly insisted that students and scholars who read and used the *I Ching* bear in mind that "the *I* was originally created for divination."[16]

> The *I* was created merely as a divination book.... Fu-hsi's and King Wen's *I* was originally created for this use. Originally it did not contain very many moral principles (*tao-li*). Only then had the original intention of the *I* not been lost. Today, people still do not understand the sage's original intention in creating the *I* -- they first want to discuss moral principles. Even though they discuss them well, they fail to situate [the *I*] in its original context. [Their writings] simply have nothing to do with the origin of the *I*. The Sage [Confucius] has clearly explained, "In antiquity the sages created the *I* by observing the images [in heaven], laying out the hexagrams, and appending the texts to them in order to elucidate good fortune and misfortune."[17] This is abundantly clear. My reason for claiming that the *I* is merely a divination book can be seen in this kind of passage....

Introduction

People reading the *I* today should divide it into three levels: Fu-hsi's *I*, King Wen's *I*, and Confucius' *I*. If one reads Fu-hsi's *I* as if there were no *T'uan*, *Hsiang*, and *Wen-yen* [appendices], then one will be able to see that the original intention of the *I* was to create the practice of divination.[18]

King Wen's mind was not as expansive as Fu-hsi's, and so he was concerned with explaining [Fu-hsi's insights]. Confucius' mind was not as great as King Wen's mind, so he too was concerned with explaining the moral principles. This is how the original intention [of the *I*] was dissipated.[19]

Chu Hsi's treatment of the *I Ching* is best understood as an effort to facilitate the individual's efforts at self-cultivation, especially in terms of what the *Great Learning* calls the "rectification of mind" (*cheng-hsin*),[20] and the practical problems entailed in moral practice -- i.e. understanding the proper response to a given set of circumstances. His work on the *I* was an attempt to make available, not only to literati but also to common people, the wisdom and transformative moral power of the sages who created the *I*.[21] Divination was the primary means by which access to this power could be attained.

This, then, was the premise for both of Chu Hsi's books on the *I*. In his commentary, the *Original Meaning of the Classic of Change* (*Chou-i pen-i*), he focuses on the *yin-yang* structure of the hexagrams, which was the medium by which Fu-hsi conveyed the ethical meanings of the original oracle. To focus attention on Fu-hsi's "original meaning" Chu published his edition of the text, with his commentary, with all the appendices intact and separate from the earlier layers of the text. It had been the general practice ever since the ascendance of Wang Pi's interpretation of the *I* to collate the *T'uan*, *Hsiang*, and *Wen-yen* commentaries (comprising five of the Ten Wings) with the hexagrams to which they applied. When Wang Pi's commentary was later enshrined in the *Chou-i cheng-i* (Correct Meaning of the *I Ching*) as the official interpretation of the T'ang Dynasty, this arrangement of the text acquired yet higher status. The most prominent *i-li* commentator of the Northern Sung, Ch'eng I, followed Wang Pi's arrangement. It was, by this time, a standard feature of the *i-li* approach -- partly because of Wang Pi's authoritative status, but mostly because the arrangement supported both the technical and the philosophical hermeneutics of the *i-li* school, according to which the meaning of the *I* is best sought in the text, not directly in the hexagrams themselves. Chu Hsi's insistence that the later levels of the *I* were of secondary importance was thus reflected in his arrangement of the text. [22]

The *I-hsüeh ch'i-meng*, Chu Hsi's second book on the *I*, was published in 1186. It is essentially an introduction to the practice of *I Ching* divination. The first of its four chapters is a detailed study of the numerological and cosmological symbolism of the *Ho-t'u* (Yellow River Chart) and the *Lo-shu* (Lo River Text). These are numerological diagrams that were said to have been revealed to Fu-hsi and the later sage-king Yao, respectively, and that had been associated with the *I Ching* ever since the Han dynasty. The *Ho-t'u*, in particular, was said to have been used by Fu-hsi as a model for the hexagrams of the *I* -- although the connections between the two are extremely vague. Chu accepted the tradition of the historical origins of these diagrams, and believed them to have been revealed to the sages by Heaven (*T'ien*); hence the need to "fathom their principles" (*ch'iung-li*). This he does in the *I-hsüeh ch'i-meng,* at some length. Nevertheless, he

Introduction

preferred the version of the myth recounting the creation of the *I* (quoted above) that gave a somewhat more active role to Fu-hsi in the creation of the *I*. This is because he saw Fu-hsi's contemplation of the "images in heaven" and the "patterns on earth" as a mythic paradigm of the "investigation of things" (*ko-wu*), a concept that played a key role in his epistemological theory.

In the second chapter of the *I-hsüeh ch'i-meng* Chu explores the *yin-yang* patterns by which the trigrams and hexagrams of the *I* may be generated by the successive recombination of solid and broken lines.[23] The *yin-yang* theory underlying the structure of the *I* is crucial to Chu's understanding of the text and its proper use in divination, because its original form and meaning was expressed simply by the solid and broken lines. He also discusses in this chapter the two standard arrangements of the trigrams (attributed to Fu-hsi and King Wen, respectively), as well as Shao Yung's *Hsien-t'ien* (Before Heaven, or *A Priori*) Chart.

The third chapter details the actual procedure by which the divination is performed, using stalks of the yarrow, or milfoil, plant (*achillea millefolium*). Chu Hsi had reconstructed this from the fragmentary version in the *Hsi-tz'u* appendix (A.9), and his version of the procedure has remained standard to this day.[24]

In the final chapter Chu explains how to derive a second hexagram from the one determined by the yarrow stalks, and how to interpret the transformation from the first to the second as a prognostication. This is how the divination system embodies a dynamic, directional aspect, or vector, thereby providing a glimpse into a potential future outcome of the present situation.

The *I-hsüeh ch'i-meng* is not among Chu Hsi's more philosophical works, but its influence should not be underestimated. It provided the standard method of *I Ching* divination for 800 years, a method that is still in use. Divination has been one of the most common forms of religious ritual in Chinese culture since the beginning of the historical record, in about 1500 BCE.[25] It often goes along with sacrifice (offerings to gods and ancestors), which is the other most common form of ritual. Divination using the *I* has been largely the practice of the aristocratic and literate classes, and today it is overshadowed in Chinese culture by other forms of popular divination.[26] But in Chinese cities today (mainly those outside of mainland China) one still sees fortune-tellers offering *I Ching* divination, and there are still Chinese (and other) intellectuals who consider it to be a useful adjunct to the process of moral self-cultivation. As a practical manual of divination, it is still being used by those dedicated to learning the "Way of the Sages."

Appendix: The Sixty-four Hexagrams

1	☰☰	*Ch'ien / Qian* (Wade-Giles / Pinyin)	The Creative (Wilhelm/Baynes trans.) Pure Yang (Lynn trans.)
2	☷☷	*K'un / Kun*	The Receptive Pure Yin
3	☵☳	*Chun / Zhun*	Difficulty at the Beginning Birth Throes
4	☶☵	*Meng*	Youthful Folly Juvenile Ignorance
5	☵☰	*Hsü / Xu*	Waiting (Nourishment)
6	☰☵	*Sung / Song*	Conflict Contention
7	☷☵	*Shih / Shi*	The Army
8	☵☷	*Pi / Bi*	Holding Together [Union] Closeness

Introduction

9	☴☰	*Hsiao-hsü / Xiaoxu*	The Taming Power of the Small Lesser Domestication
10	☰☱	*Lü*	Treading [Conduct]
11	☷☰	*T'ai / Tai*	Peace
12	☰☷	*P'i / Pi*	Standstill [Stagnation] Obstruction
13	☰☲	*T'ung-jen / Tongren*	Fellowship with Men Fellowship
14	☲☰	*Ta-yu / Dayou*	Possession in Great Measure Great Holdings
15	☷☶	*Ch'ien / Qian*	Modesty
16	☳☷	*Yü / Yu*	Enthusiasm Contentment

Introduction

17	䷐	*Sui*	Following
18	䷑	*Ku / Gu*	Work on what has been spoiled [Decay] Ills to be Cured
19	䷒	*Lin*	Approach Overseeing
20	䷓	*Kuan / Guan*	Contemplation (View) Viewing
21	䷔	*Shih-ho / Shihe*	Biting Through Bite Together
22	䷕	*Pi / Bi*	Grace Elegance
23	䷖	*Po / Bo*	Splitting Apart Peeling
24	䷗	*Fu*	Return (The Turning Point)

Introduction

25	䷘	*Wu-wang / Wuwang*	Innocence (The Unexpected) No Errancy
26	䷙	*Ta-hsu / Daxu*	The Taming Power of the Great Great Domestication
27	䷚	*I / Yi*	Corners of the Mouth Nourishment
28	䷛	*Ta-kuo / Daguo*	Preponderance of the Great Major Superiority
29	䷜	*K'an / Xikan*	The Abysmal (Water) The Constant Sinkhole
30	䷝	*Li*	The Clinging, Fire Cohesion
31	䷞	*Hsien / Xian*	Influence (Wooing) Reciprocity
32	䷟	*Heng*	Duration Perseverance

xv

Introduction

33	䷠	*Tun / Dun*	Retreat Withdrawl
34	䷡	*Ta-chuang / Dazhuang*	The Power of the Great Great Strength
35	䷢	*Chin / Jin*	Progress Advance
36	䷣	*Ming-i / Mingyi*	Darkening of the Light Suppression of the Light
37	䷤	*Chia-jen / Jiaren*	The Family [The Clan]
38	䷥	*K'uei / Kui*	Opposition Contrariety
39	䷦	*Chien / Jian*	Obstruction Adversity
40	䷧	*Hsieh / Xie*	Deliverance Release

Introduction

41	䷨	*Sun*	Decrease Diminution
42	䷩	*I / Yi*	Increase
43	䷪	*K'uai / Kuai*	Break-through (Resoluteness) Resolution
44	䷫	*Kou / Gou*	Coming to Meet Encounter
45	䷬	*Ts'ui / Cui*	Gathering Together [Massing] Gathering
46	䷭	*Sheng*	Pushing Upward Climbing
47	䷮	*K'un / Kun*	Oppression (Exhaustion) Impasse
48	䷯	*Ching / Jing*	The Well

xvii

Introduction

49	䷰	*Ko / Ge*	Revolution (Molting) Radical Change
50	䷱	*Ting / Ding*	The Cauldron
51	䷲	*Chen / Zhen*	The Arousing (Shock, Thunder) Quake
52	䷳	*Ken / Gen*	Keeping Still, Mountain Restraint
53	䷴	*Chien / Jian*	Development (Gradual Progress) Gradual Advance
54	䷵	*Kuei-mei / Guimei*	The Marrying Maiden Marrying Maid
55	䷶	*Feng*	Abundance [Fullness]
56	䷷	*Lü*	The Wanderer

Introduction

57	Sun	The Gentle (Penetrating, Wind) / Compliance
58	Tui / Dui	The Joyous, Lake / Joy
59	Huan	Dispersion [Dissolution]
60	Chieh / Jie	Limitation / Control
61	Chung-fu / Zhongfu	Inner Truth / Inner Trust
62	Hsiao-kuo / Xiaoguo	Preponderance of the Small / Minor Superiority
63	Chi-chi / Jiji	After Completion / Ferrying Complete
64	Wei-chi / Weiji	Before Completion / Ferrying Incomplete

Introduction

---

1. This introduction is based on Kidder Smith, Jr., Peter K. Bol, Joseph A. Adler, and Don J. Wyatt, *Sung Dynasty Uses of the I Ching* (Princeton: Princeton University Press, 1990), ch. 6, and Joseph A. Adler, *Divination and Philosophy: Chu Hsi's Understanding of the* I-ching (Ph.D. dissertation: University of California at Santa Barbara, 1984).

2. The Eight Trigrams (*pa-kua*) are:

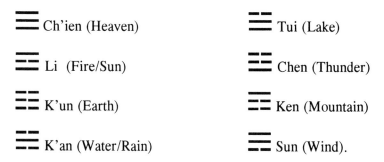

☰ Ch'ien (Heaven)   ☱ Tui (Lake)

☲ Li (Fire/Sun)   ☳ Chen (Thunder)

☷ K'un (Earth)   ☶ Ken (Mountain)

☵ K'an (Water/Rain)   ☴ Sun (Wind).

The 64 Hexagrams, or six-line diagrams, can be derived by combining the trigrams in all possible pairs. They each have a name reflecting the overall *yin-yang* structure; each is thought to represent an "archetype" of a social or natural situation in which the questioner can be involved. In the method of divination explained by Chu Hsi in the *I-hsüeh ch'i-meng*, the subject derives a second hexagram from the first, thereby yielding 4,096 (64^2) possible situations. It is impossible to determine a date of origin of the hexagrams or trigrams, although they may very well go back to the beginning of the Chou dynasty in the eleventh century BCE, or even earlier.

The older parts of the basic texts commenting on each hexagram (*kua-tz'u*, or hexagram statements) cannot be dated with any confidence; these are the divinatory formulas, such as "auspicious," "inauspicious," "beneficial," etc. The later parts of the hexagram statements may date from the 9th c. BCE. See Iulian K. Shchutskii, *Researches on the I Ching* (Princeton: Princeton University Press, 1979), pp. 181-195; Arthur Waley, "The Book of Changes," *Bulletin of the Museum of Far Eastern Antiquities*, 5 (1933), pp. 121-142; Richard John Lynn, trans., *The Classic of Changes: A New Translation of the I Ching as Interpreted by Wang Bi* (New York: Columbia University Press, 1994), Introduction; and Edward L. Shaughnessy, trans., *I Ching: The Classic of Changes* (New York: Ballantine Books, 1996), Introduction.

3. The Ten Wings were probably compiled from roughly the 6th century BCE to the 1st century CE. It should also be mentioned that the *I Ching* is a foundational text of the Taoist religion too, and is accepted and used by Chinese Buddhists as well. But here we are concerned with the *I Ching* as a Confucian text.

4. Mencius (Meng Tzu) lived in the 4th century BCE and developed the political, psychological, and ethical dimensions of Confucius' thought. He is especially known for his theory that human nature is inherently good. See D.C. Lau, trans., *Mencius* (Harmondsworth: Penguin, 1970).

5. The chief representatives of eleventh-century thought that Chu Hsi included in his synthesis were Chou Tun-i (1017-1073), Chang Tsai (1020-1077), and the brothers Ch'eng Hao (1032-1085) and Ch'eng I (1033-1107) (see Wing-tsit Chan, comp., *A Source Book in Chinese Philosophy* [Princeton: Princeton University Press, 1963], chs. 28-32). These figures constituted what was known at the time as the Ch'eng school, and after Chu Hsi became known as the Ch'eng-Chu school, or *Tao-hsüeh* (The Learning of the Way). It is important to bear in mind that the Ch'eng school did not constitute the entirety of eleventh-century Confucian thought, and that Chu's synthesis was a selective one. See Hoyt Cleveland Tillman, *Confucian Discourse and Chu Hsi's Ascendancy* (Honolulu: University of Hawaii Press, 1992).

Introduction

6. See Ch'en Chen-sun (fl. 1211-1249), *Chih-chai shu-lu chieh-t'i* (Annotated Bibliography of Chih-chai Library) (Kuo-hsüeh chi-pen ts'ung-shu, vol. 3). ch.1; Wang Mou-hung, *Chu-tzu nien-p'u* (Biography of Chu Hsi) (1706; rpt. Taipei: Shih-chieh, 1966), p. 280; *Ssu-k'u ch'üan-shu ts'ung-mu t'i-yao* (Summaries of Works in the Imperial Library) (Kuo-hsüeh chi-pen ts'ung-shu ed.), vol. 1, ch. 3, pp. 27-28; and Toda Toyosabur ,*Ekky Ch shaku Shik* (Outline History *of I Ching* Commentaries) (Tokyo: Fugen, 1968), pp. 581-593.

The *Chou-i pen-i* has been reprinted and is available in numerous editions; the *I-hsüeh ch'i-meng* in somewhat fewer. Editions of the *Chou-i pen-i* include the Imperial Academy edition (rpt. Taipei: Hua-lien, 1978), and Li Kuang-ti, ed., *Chou-i che-chung* (The *I Ching* Judged Evenly) (1715; rpt. Taipei: Chen Shan Mei, 1971), 2 vols. In the latter, Chu's commentary is collated with Ch'eng I's *I-chuan* (Commentary on the *I*).

The editions of the *I-hsüeh ch'i-meng* chiefly consulted for this translation are those contained in the *Chou-i che-chung* (both the Chen Shan Mei and the Ssu-k'u ch'üan-shu editions), and an edition pubished in 1975 by Kuang-hsüeh Publishers (Taipei). Other editions include *Chu-tzu i-shu* (Chu Hsi's Surviving Works) (rpt. Taipei, 1969), vol. 12; Hu Kuang, comp., *Hsing-li ta-ch'üan shu* (Great Compendium on Nature and Principle) (1415; rpt. Ssu-k'u ch'üan-shu chen-pen, 5th series), chs. 14-17; and Li Kuang-ti, comp., *Hsing-li ching-i* (Essential Meanings of Nature and Principle) (1715; rpt. Ssu-pu pei-yao ed.), ch. 4.

Besides these two books there are numerous essays and letters in Chu Hsi's Collected Papers (*Chu wen-kung wen-chi*) concerning the *I*, and a surprisingly large section of his Classified Conversations (*Chu-tzu yü-lei*) is devoted to the *I*: approximately 11% of the total number of pages.

7. The other two were Shen-nung ("Divine Farmer"), who invented agriculture, and Huang-ti ("Yellow Emperor"), the first political ruler, under whose rule were invented writing, sericulture, boats, carts, and the bow and arrow.

8. Chu believed that at some later time Fu-hsi combined the trigrams into hexagrams.

9. *Hsi-tz'u* B.2.1. Citations to the *Hsi-tz'u* refer to Chu Hsi's version, which was also used by Legge and Wilhelm in their translations of the *I Ching*. The placement of some passages differs from the Wang Bi / Han K'ang-po text, which was used by Lynn in his translation and by the Harvard-Yenching Institute Sinological Index Series, supplement no. 10: *A Concordance to Yi Ching* (Taipei, 1966). The *Hsi-tz'u* is also called the *Ta-chuan* (Great Treatise, or Great Appendix).

For Chu's discussion of the relationship between this myth and the one involving the *Ho-t'u* (Yellow River Chart), see *Chou-i che-chung*, p. 1207 (Chu's reply to Yüan-shu).

10. See D. C. Lau, trans., *Mencius*, book 6, part A.

11. See Tu Wei-ming, *Centrality and Commonality: An Essay on Confucian Religiousness* (Albany: SUNY Press, 1989). Other examples of this principle include the claim made by the *Li-chi* (Record of Ritual), one of the Five Classics, that the ritual forms "represent the distinctions of Heaven and Earth" (Fung Yu-lan, *A History of Chinese Philosophy*, 2nd ed. [Cambridge: Harvard University Press, 1952], trans. Derk Bodde, vol. 1, p. 344); and the first line of the *Hsi-tz'u* (Appended Remarks) appendix of the *I Ching*, which says, "As Heaven is high and noble and earth is low and humble, so it is that Ch'ien and K'un are defined. The high and the low being thereby set out, the exalted and the mean [in society] have their places accordingly" (trans. of *Hsi-tz'u* A.1.1 by Richard John Lynn in *The Classic of Changes*, p. 47).

Introduction

12. These are called *t'uan* (judgments, decisions), or *kua-tz'u* (hexagram statements).

13. These are called *yao-tz'u*, or line statements.

14. The Ten Wings actually comprise only eight texts, because two are in two parts. They are:

   1) *T'uan chuan* (in two parts): commentary on the hexagram texts.
   2) *Ta-hsiang chuan* (Greater Image commentary): symbolism of the hexagrams in terms of their component trigrams.
   3) *Hsiao-hsiang chuan* (Smaller Image commentary): symbolism of each line.
   4) *Wen-yen chuan* (Words of the Text): commentary on hexagrams 1 and 2.
   5) *Hsi-tz'u chuan* (Appended Remarks, also known as the *Ta-chuan*, or Great Treatise, in two parts): general treatise on the cosmological principles underlying the *Classic of Change*.
   6) *Shuo-kua chuan* (Comments on the Trigrams): comments on the symbolism of the trigrams (plus some sections very much like the *Hsi-tz'u*).
   7) *Hsü-kua chuan* (Sequence of the Hexagrams): a mnemonic verse for remembering the sequence of hexagrams in the text.
   8) *Tsa-kua chuan* (Hexagram Miscellany): miscellaneous remarks.

For a fuller discussion of the Ten Wings, see Iulian K. Shchutskii, *Researches on the I Ching*, pp. 158-165.

15. These two diagrams are the subject of the first chapter of the *I-hsüeh ch'i-meng*.

16. See, e.g., *Chu-tzu yü-lei*, ch. 66, *passim*.

17. *Hsi-tz'u* A.2.1, slightly reworded.

18. *Chu-tzu yü-lei* 66, p. 2591.

19. Ibid., pp. 2592-93.

20. See Wing-tsit Chan, *Source Book*, p. 86.

21. The ability to "transform" (*hua*) others was a traditional hallmark of the Confucian sage. See, e.g., *Mencius* 7A.13, "the superior person transforms where he passes."

22. Nevertheless, this arrangement was not retained in all later editions of Chu Hsi's commentary.

23. This is an alternative method of deriving the sixty-four hexagrams, useful for understanding their *yin-yang* relationships, but it is not how Fu-hsi derived them, according to Chu.

24. It is the one given in the Richard Wilhelm/Cary F. Baynes translation of the *I* (*The I Ching, or Book of Changes*, 3rd ed. [Princeton: Princeton University Press, 1967], pp. 721-723; and in Richard John Lynn, *The Classic of Changes*, pp. 19-21.

25. Divination using the *I* was preceded by oracle-bone divination in the court of the Shang dynasty (17th–11th c. BCE), which gradually faded from use during the Chou period.

26. These include the use of *shen-pei*, or "moon blocks;" *ch'ien*, or divination slips; and *chi-t'ung*, or spirit-mediums.

Introduction to the Study of the *Classic of Change*

易學啟蒙

by Chu Hsi

朱熹

Preface

The Sage [Fu-hsi] contemplated the images in order to draw the diagrams, and cast the yarrow stalks in order to determine the lines.[1] This enables all people of later ages throughout the world to decide uncertainty and doubt, to settle indecision, and to be undeluded about following the auguries "auspicious," "inauspicious," "repentance" and "regret."[2] This achievement can be called glorious.

Thus the hexagrams, from root to trunk and from trunk to branch, have such compelling power they cannot stop.[3] The yarrow stalks divide and combine, advance and retreat, follow and unite; horizontally and vertically, backwards and forwards -- and there is no movement that is not well-ordered. How could this have been achieved by the Sage's cogitation and wise deliberation?[4] It was simply the naturalness of a particular phase of *ch'i*, formed into the patterns and images seen in the Chart and Text, that exposed this to his mind, and he lent his hand to it.

Students of recent ages seem to be fond of discussing the *I*, but have not examined this point. Those who specialize in the meaning of the text,[5] their branches distantly scattered and dispersed, have no concreteness in their writings. Those who are versed in the images and numbers[6] are all bound by forced associations,[7] and some consider them to have come from the Sage's cogitation and wise deliberation. This being the case, I am grieved by it.

Therefore, with my colleague [Ts'ai Yüan-ting[8]] I have gathered together the old sayings[9] into a book of four sections, in order to show beginning students how to engage without doubts in their discussions.

易學啟蒙

聖人觀象以畫卦，揲蓍以命爻，使天下後世之人，皆有以決嫌疑，定猶豫，而不迷於吉凶悔吝之途，其功可謂盛矣。

然其為卦也，自本而幹，自幹而枝，其勢若有所迫而自不能已。其為蓍也，分合進退，從衡逆順，亦無往而不相值焉。是豈聖人心思智慮之所得為也哉。特氣數之自然，形於法象，見於圖書者，有以啟於其心而假手焉爾。

近世學者，類喜談易而不察乎此。其專於文義者，既支離散漫，而無所根著。其涉於象數者，又皆牽合傅會，而或以為出於聖人心思智慮之所為也。若是者予竊病焉。

因與同志，頗輯舊聞，為書四篇，以示初學，使毋疑於其說云。

Personally recorded by the True Recluse of Yün-t'ai [Temple][10] on the 15th day of the last month of spring in the *ping-wu* year of Ch'un-hsi [1186].[11]

淳熙丙午暮春既望　臺真逸手記。

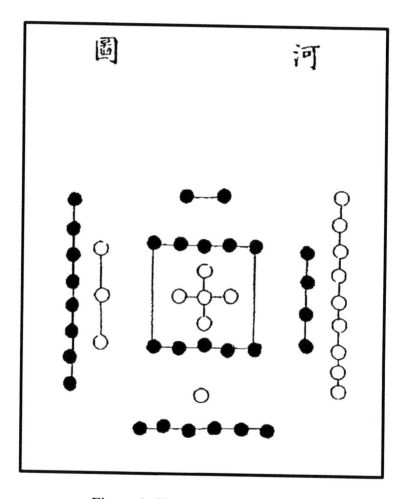

Figure 1: The River Chart (*Ho-t'u*)

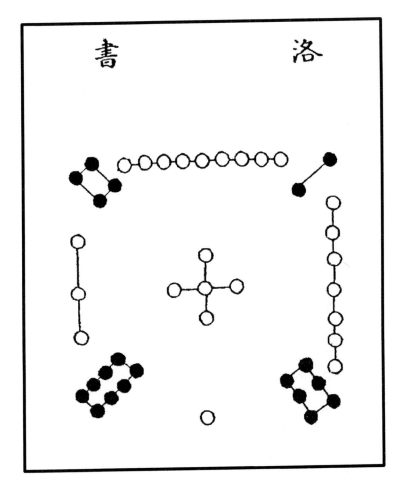

Figure 2: The Lo Text (*Lo-shu*)

I. The Original "Chart" and "Text"[12]

The "Great Treatise"[13] of the *Changes* says:
The River gave forth the Chart, and the Lo gave forth the Text. The Sage(s) took them as models.[14]

K'ung An-kuo [second century BCE] said:

The River Chart came out of the Yellow River on a dragon-horse when Fu-hsi ruled the world. He accordingly took its design as a model and drew the Eight Trigrams. The Lo Text was the design arrayed on the back of a spirit-tortoise in the time when Yü controlled the waters. In it are the numbers up to 9. Yü accordingly followed its classifications in completing the Nine Divisions [of the world].[15]

Liu Hsin[16] said:

Fu-hsi ruled according to Heaven. He received the River Chart and drew it; this became the Eight Trigrams. Yü controlled the flooding waters. He was bestowed the Lo Text and arranged its patterns into the Nine Divisions. The River Chart and the Lo Text relate to each other as warp and woof. The Eight Trigrams and Nine Divisions relate to each other as inside and outside.[17]

Kuan Tzu-ming[18] said:

The design of the River Chart is 7 in front, 6 behind, 8 on the left, and 9 on the right. The design of the Lo Text is 9 in front, 1 in the rear, 3 on the left, 7 on the right, 4 in the left-front, 2 in the right-front, 8 in the left-rear, and 6 in the right-rear.

Master Shao [Yung][19] said:

本圖書第一

易大傳曰:河出圖,洛出書,聖人則之。

孔安國云:

河圖者,伏羲氏王天下,龍馬出河。遂則其文,以畫八卦。洛書者,禹治水時,神龜負文而列於背。有數至九,禹遂因而第之,以成九類。

劉歆云:

伏羲氏繼天而王。受河圖而畫之,八卦是也。禹治洪水。錫洛書,法而陳之,九疇是也。河圖洛書相為經緯。八卦九章,相為表裏。

關子明云:

河圖之文,七前六後,八左九右。洛書之文,九前一後。三左七右。四前左,二前右,八後左,六後右。

The circle is the [movement of the] stars. The numbers of the calendrical record are founded on this.[20]

> [Ts'ai Yüan-ting:] The calendrical methods combine the first two lines [of the hexagrams] in determining the firm and yielding; the two middle lines in determining the tones and calendars; the two final lines in recording the intercalary period. This is what is meant by "calendrical record."[21]

[Shao continued:] The square is Earth. The method of drawing the Divisions and well-field plots is copied from this.[22]

> [Ts'ai Yüan-ting:] There were nine Divisions, and each well-field had 900 *mu*.[23] This is what is meant by "drawing the Divisions and well-field plots."

[Shao continued:] The circle refers to the River Chart's numbers, and the square to the Lo Text's design. Thus Fu-hsi and King Wen based on this [the circle] their creation of the Changes,[24] and Yü, according to Chi,[25] used this [the square] in making the Great Plan.[26]

> Ts'ai Yüan-ting says: Ancient and modern biographers, from K'ung An-kuo, Liu Hsiang and his son, and Pan Ku, all consider that the River Chart was given to [Fu] Hsi, and the Lo Text conferred on Yü. Kuan Tzu-ming and Shao K'ang-chieh [Shao Yung] both use ten [numbers] for the River Chart and nine [numbers] for the Lo Text. These are the number 55 [the sum of the numbers 1 through 10] by which the "Great Treatise" arranges Heaven and Earth, and the numbers of the 9 Regions and 9 Offices of the Great Plan, which the Great Plan [chapter]

邵子曰：

圓者星也。歷紀之數，其肇於此乎。

〔蔡元定〕歷法合二始以定剛柔，二中以定律歷，二終以紀閏餘。是所謂歷紀也。

〔邵子〕方者土也。畫州井地之法，其倣於此乎。

〔蔡元定〕州有九井九百畝，是所謂畫州井地也。

〔邵子〕蓋圓者河圖之數，方者洛書之文。故羲文因之而造易，禹箕敘之而作範也。

蔡元定曰：古今傳紀，自孔安國，劉向父子，班固，皆以為河圖授羲，洛書錫禹。關子明，邵康節，皆以十為河圖，九為洛書。蓋大傳既陳天地五十有五之數，洪範又明言天乃錫禹洪

> numbers of the 9 Regions and 9 Offices of the Great Plan, which the Great Plan [chapter] explains was conferred on Yü by Heaven. With 9 at its head and 1 at its tail, 3 on the left and 7 on the right, 2 and 4 as shoulders and 6 and 8 as feet, [the Lo Text is] an accurate image of the back of a tortoise. Only in Liu Mu's opinion is 9 the River Chart and 10 the Lo Text. He attributes these to Hsi-i [Ch'en T'uan].[27]

Since the old theories of various scholars do not agree, we follow the "Great Treatise" and consider both [diagrams] to have appeared in Fu-hsi's time. The *I* is founded on the Chart and the Text. Neither is explained; it is only said that Fu-hsi drew from both the Chart and Text.[28]

That the numbers of the *I* and the [Great] Plan are really "outside and inside" is doubtful.[29] In fact, the principle of Heaven and Earth is simply one. Although in terms of time there is a difference between old and new, or before and after, nevertheless the principle does not admit of duality. Therefore Fu-hsi was merely assisted by the River Chart in creating the *I*; it was not necessary for him previously to have seen the Lo Text and duplicate it. The Great Yü was merely assisted by the Lo Text in creating the Plan; it was not necessary for him to go back to examine the River Chart and match it.[30]

How did they [the Chart and Text] come to be what they are? Because outside this principle there is no other principle. But it is not only this. The pitch-pipes have 5 sounds and 12 pipes, and multiplied together they come to 60. The names of the days have 10 stems and 12 branches, and taken together they also come to 60.[31] These two both appeared after the *I*, and the numbers that they evince are not the

範九疇而九宮之數。戴九履一，左三右七，二四為肩，六八為足，正龜背之象也。惟劉牧臆見，以九為河圖，十為洛書。托言出於希夷。

既與諸儒舊說不合，又引大傳，以為者皆出於伏羲之世。其易置圖畫，並無明驗，但謂伏羲兼取圖畫。

則易範之數，誠相表裏，為可疑耳。其實天地之理，一而已矣。雖時有古今先後之不同而其理則不容於有二也。故伏羲但據河圖以作易，則不必豫見洛書，而已逆與之合矣。大禹但據洛畫以作範，則亦不必追考河圖，而已暗與之符矣。

其所以然者何哉？誠以此理之外，無復它理故也。然不特此爾。律呂有五聲十二律，而其相乘之數，究於六十。日名有十乾十二

60, with [virtually] no disagreement, just like tally slips. And finally, things like the circulating *ch'i*, the Kinship of the Three [*Ts'an-t'ung*], and the Supreme One [T'ai-i], although not quite the [Confucian] Tao, are also mutually consistent.[32] They are all natural principle. Even if we were to command the Chart and Text to appear again today, their numbers would have to match [the originals]. We can say [therefore] that Fu-hsi "took from today"[33] in creating the *I*. The passage in the Great Treatise – "The [Yellow] River gave forth the Chart, the Lo [River] gave forth the Text, and the Sage(s) copied them"[34] – speaks in general terms of the Sage(s) creating the *I* and creating the Plan. They both [in fact] originated from the intention of Heaven [*t'ien chih i*]. Other examples are such sayings as "[The Sages] valued its prognostications in their divination,"[35] and "There is nothing greater than the milfoil and the tortoise."[36] How can the *Classic of Change* contain the tortoise method of divination [as well as the milfoil]? In speaking of principle there is simply no duality.

> **Heaven is 1, Earth is 2; Heaven is 3, Earth is 4; Heaven is 5, Earth is 6; Heaven is 7, Earth is 8; Heaven is 9, Earth is 10. There are five numbers of Heaven and five numbers of Earth. The five positions match each other and each has its mate. The numbers of Heaven equal 25; the numbers of Earth equal 30. Altogether the numbers of Heaven and Earth equal 55. This is what completes the changes and transformations and activates the ghosts and spirits.**[37]

This section is the one in which Confucius explained the numbers of the River Chart. Between Heaven and Earth there is the unitary *ch'i*. This divides into two, making *yin* and

支,而其相乘之數,亦究於六十。二者皆出於易之後,其起數又各不同。然與易之陰陽策數多少自相配合。皆為六十者無不合若符契也。下至運氣參同太乙之屬。雖不足道,然亦無不相通,蓋自然之理也。假令今世復有圖畫者出,其數亦必相符。可謂伏羲有取於今日而作易乎。大傳所謂河出圖,洛出書,聖人則之者,亦汎言聖人作易作範。其原皆出於天之意。如言以卜筮者尚其占。與莫大乎:蓍龜之類。易之書豈有龜與卜之法乎?亦言其理無二而已爾。

> 天一地二,天三地四,天五地六,天七地八,天九地十。天數五,地數五。五位相得,而各有合。天數二十有五,地數三十。凡天地之數五十有五。此所以成變化而行鬼神也。

此一節夫子所以發明河圖之數也。天地之間,一氣而已。分而為二,則為陰陽。而五

yang. Yet in the Five Phases and the production and transformation of the myriad things, from first to last there is nothing that is not governed by this [principle].

Therefore as for the positions of the River Chart: 1 and 6 are akin and reside in the north;[38] 2 and 7 are friends and reside in the south; 3 and 8 are similar and reside in the east; 4 and 9 are cohorts and reside in the west; 5 and 10 protect each other and reside in the center. This is because as numbers they are nothing more than "one *yin*, one *yang*," each pair [corresponding] with one of the Five Phases.[39]

What we call Heaven is the light purity of *yang*, which positions itself upward. What we call Earth is the heavy turbidity of *yin*, which positions itself downward. The *yang* numbers are odd. Thus 1, 3, 5, 7 and 9 are all classified as Heavenly. This is what is meant by the "five numbers of Heaven." The *yin* numbers are even; thus 2, 4, 6, 8 and 10 are all classified as Earthly. This is what is meant by the "five numbers of Earth." The Heavenly numbers and Earthly numbers each according to their kind attract each other. This is what is meant by the statement, "The five positions match each other." Heaven from 1 gives rise to water, and Earth with 6 completes it. Earth from 2 gives rise to fire, and Heaven with 7 completes it. Heaven from 3 gives rise to wood, and Earth with 8 completes it. Earth from 4 gives rise to metal, and Heaven with 9 completes it. Heaven from 5 gives rise to soil, and Earth with 10 completes it. This is the meaning of "Each has its mate." Summing up the five odds we get 25; summing up the five evens we get 30. Together these two make 55. This is the complete number of the River Chart, according to both the ideas of Confucius and the discourses of all the scholars.

行造化，萬物始終，無不管於是焉。

故河圖之位。一與六共宗而居乎北。二與七為朋而居乎南。三與八同道而居乎東。四與九為友而居乎西。五與十相守而居乎中。蓋其所以為數者，不過一陰一陽，一兩其五行而已。所謂天者陽之輕清而位乎上者也。

所謂地者，陰之重濁而位乎下者也。陽數奇，故一三五七皆屬乎天，所謂天數五＂也。陰數偶，故二四六八十皆屬乎地，所謂地數五也。天數地數各以類而相求，所謂五位之相得者然也。天以一生水，而地以六成之。地以二生火，而天以七成之。天以三生木，而地以八成之。地以四生金，而天以九成之。天以五生土，而地以十成之。此又其所謂各有合焉者也。積五奇而為二十五，積五耦而為三十。合是二者而為五十有五。此河圖之全數，皆夫子之意，而諸儒之說也。

As for the Lo Text, although Confucius did not speak of it, still the diagram and the explanation had already been written down earlier. If there is anything with which we can penetrate them, then what Liu Hsin said about he warp and woof, outside and inside, can reveal it.

Someone asked: Why is it that the positions and numbers in the River Chart and the Lo Text are not the same?

Answer: The River Chart connects the five generative numbers [1-5] with the five completing numbers [6-10], situating them together in each direction. By revealing them together to people it gives order to their constant [principles]; this is the substance of number. The Lo Text connects the five odd numbers with the four even numbers, putting each in its place. By emphasizing the *yang* in control of the *yin*, it initiates their changes; this is the functioning of number.

Question: Why do they both place 5 in the center?

[Answer:] The beginning of all numbers is simply "One *yin*, one *yang*." The symbol of *yang* is the circle. If the circle's diameter is 1 its circumference is 3. The symbol of *yin* is the square. If the square's side is 1, its perimeter is 4. If a circumference is 3, and we take 1 as 1, by tripling this 1 *yang* [diameter] we make it 3. If a perimeter is 4, and we take 2 as 1, by doubling the 1 *yin* [side] we make it 2. This is what is meant by "Triple Heaven and double Earth."[40] 3 and 2 together then make 5. This is why the numbers of the River Chart and the Lo Text both place 5 at the center.

至于洛書，則雖夫子之所未言，然其象其說，已具於前。有以通之，則劉歆所謂經緯表裏者可見矣。

或曰：河圖洛書之位與數，其所以不同何也？

曰：河圖以五生數統五成數而同處。其蓋揭其全以示人，而道其常，數之體也。洛書以五奇數統四偶數，而各居其所。蓋主於陽以統陰而肇其變，數之用也。

曰：其皆以五居中者何也？

凡數之始，一陰一陽而已矣。陽之象圖，圓者經一而圍三。陰之象方，方者經一而圍四。圍三者以一為一，故參其一陽而為三。圍四者以二為一，故兩其一陰而為二。是所謂參天兩地者也。三二之合則為五矣。此河圖洛書之數，所以皆以五為中也。

However, the River Chart takes generative numbers as primary. Therefore the reason for its center being 5 is also that it contains the symbols of the five generative numbers in it. The dot below is the image of the 1 of Heaven. The dots above are the image of the 2 of Earth. The dots to the left are the image of the 3 of Heaven. The dots to the right are the image of the 4 of Earth. The dots in the center are the image of the 5 of Heaven.

The Lo Text takes odd numbers as primary. Therefore the reason for its center being 5 is also that it contains the images of the five odd numbers in it. The dot below is the image of the 1 of Heaven. The dots on the left are the image of the 3 of Heaven. The dots in the center are the image of the 5 of Heaven. The dots on the right are the image of the 7 of Heaven. The dots above are the image of the 9 of Heaven. The numbers in relation to their positions include three that are the same [as the River Chart: 1, 3, and 5] and two that are different [7 and 9]. This is because *yang* [i.e., 3] cannot change, while *yin* [2] can change. Completing numbers, although *yang*, are certainly the *yin* of generative numbers.

Question: Since the central 5 is the image of the five numbers, how is it a number?

Answer: Speaking of it as number, it pervades the whole Chart. From inside to outside each is certainly a number with a sum that can be recorded. Yet, the 1, 2, 3, and 4 of the

然河圖以生數為主，故其中之所以為五者，亦具五生數之象焉。其下一點，天一之象也。其上一點，地二之象也。其左一點，天三之象也。其右一點，地四之象也。其中一點，天五之象也。

洛書以奇數為主，故其中之所以為五者，亦具五奇數之象焉。其下一點，亦天一之象也。其左一點，亦天三之象也。其中一點，亦天五之象也。其右一點，則天七之象也。其上一點，則天九之象也。其數與位，皆三同而二異。蓋陽不可易，而陰可易。成數雖陽，固亦生之陰也。

曰：中央之五，既為五數之象矣，然其為數也奈何？

曰：以數言之，通乎一圖。由內及外，固各有積實可紀之數矣。然河圖之一二三四，各居其五象。本方之外，而六七八九十者，又各因五而得數，以附於其生數之外。

River Chart each resides in the image of 5. Outside the basic square, the 6, 7, 8, 9, and 10 also each rely on the 5 to become the numbers they are, and thereby append to the outside of the generative numbers.

The 1, 3, 7, and 9 of the Lo Text also each reside in the image of 5. Outside the basic square, the 2, 4, 6, and 8 each relies on its kind, and thereby appends to the sides of the odd numbers. Thus, the middle is host and the outside is guest; the standard is ruler and the off-center is subject. So all is in order with no confusion.

Question: Why are they not the same in amounts?

Answer: The River Chart emphasizes the whole. It therefore goes up to 10, and the number of places for the odd and the even are equal. Only when discussing their sums do we see that the evens are greater and the odds are fewer.[41]

The Lo Text stresses change. It therefore goes up to 9, and its [number of] positions and its sums are both greater for the even and less for the odd. It is necessary to empty both [diagrams] in the center to make the numbers of *yin* and *yang* both be 20, with no remainder.[42]

Question: Why is it that their sequences are not the same?

Answer: When we speak of the River Chart in the cosmogonic sequence, it begins at the bottom [1], moves to

洛書之一三七，亦各居其五象。木方之外，而二四六八者，又各因其類，以附於奇數之側。蓋中者為主，而外者為客。正者為君，而側者為臣。亦各有條而不紊也。

曰：其多寡之不同何也？

曰：河圖主全，故極於十，而奇偶之位均。論其積實，然後見其耦贏而奇乏也。

洛書主變，故極於九，而其位與實皆奇贏而耦乏也。必皆虛其中也，然後陰陽之數均於二十而無偏耳。

曰：其序之不同何也？

曰：河圖以生出之次言之，則始下，次上，次左，次右，以復於中，而又始於下也。以運行之次言之，則始東，次南，次中，次西，次北，左旋一周而又始於東也。其生數之在內者，則陽居下左而陰居上右也。其成

I-hsüeh ch'i-meng

the top [2], then to the left [3], then the right [4], returning to the center [5] and beginning again at the bottom.[43] In the circulation sequence, we say it begins in the East [wood], goes next to the South [fire], then the Center [earth], then West [metal], then North [water], and then revolves leftward one circle to begin again in the East.[44] In terms of its generative numbers on the inside, *yang* is below [1] and to the left [3], *yin* is above [2] and to the right [4]. In terms of its completion numbers on the outside, *yin* is on the bottom [6] and left [8], and *yang* is on the top [7] and right [9].

In the Lo Text sequence, its *yang* numbers are first in the North [1], then the East [3], then Center [5], then West [7], and then South [9]. Its *yin* numbers are first in the Southwest [2], then Southeast [4], then Northwest [6], then Northeast [8]. Speaking of them together, they begin in the North [1] and move to the Southwest [2], then East [3], then Southeast [4], then the Center [5], then Northwest [6], then West [7], then Northeast [8], and finally South [9]. In its circulating movement, Water subdues Fire, Fire subdues Metal, Metal subdues Wood, and Wood subdues Earth, then turning one revolution to the right Earth subdues Water.[45] Thus each has its explanation.

Question: Why are the numbers 7, 8, 9 and 6 not the same [in position]?[46]

Answer: In the River Chart, 6, 7, 8, and 9 are appended to the outside of the generative numbers. This is the correct [pattern] of the mature and young *yin* and *yang*'s advancing and retreating in abundance and poverty [ie., waxing and waning]. The 9 is the sum of the generative numbers 1, 3 and 5. Thus from the north to the east and from the east to the west it thereby comes to completion outside the 4. The 6 is

數之在外者,則陰居下左,而陽居上右也。

　洛書之次,其陽數則首北,次東,次中,次西,次南;其陰數,則首西南,次東南,次西北,次東北也。合而言之,則首北,次西南,次東,次東南,次中,次西北,次西,次東北,而究於南也。其運行,則水克火,火克金,金克木,木克土,右旋一周而土復克水也。是亦各有說矣。

　曰:其七八九六之數不同何也?

　曰:河圖六七八九,既附於生數之外矣。此陰陽老少進退饒乏之正也。其九者,生數一三五之積也。故自北而東,自東而西,以成於四之外。其六者,生數二四之積也。故

the sum of the generative numbers 2 and 4. Thus from the south to the west and from the west to the north it thereby comes to completion outside the 1. The 7 results from the 9 going from the west to the south, and the 8 results from the 6 going from the north to the east. This is alternation of the mature and young *yin* and *yang*'s containment of each other.

In the vertical and horizontal 15s of the Lo Text, the 7, 8, 9, and 6 [the four key numbers of the divination method] alternately become smaller and larger. Eliminating the 5 distinguishes the 10s, so 1 implies 9, 2 implies 8, 3 implies 7, and 4 implies 6, joining in every combination; wherever they go they meet their mates. This is what makes the unlimited changes and transformations marvelous.

Question: So then, what about the Sage's using them as models?

Answer: Modeling the River Chart, he eliminated its center. Modeling the Lo Text, he combined its quantities.[47] The empty 5 and 10 of the River Chart are the Supreme Polarity (*t'ai-chi*). The odd number [sum of] 20 and the even number [sum of] 20 are the Two Modes. Taking the 1, 2, 3, and 4 along with the 6, 7, 8, and 9, they are the Four Images.[48] Dividing what fills the Four Directions, we consider them to be Heaven, Earth, Fire and Water [trigrams]. Filling the space in the four corners, we consider them to be Lake, Thunder, Wind, and Mountain. These are the 8 Trigrams.

As for the amounts of the Lo Text, the 1 is the 5 Phases, the 2 is the 5 Activities, the 3 is the 8 Objects of Government, the 4 is the 5 Periods, the 5 is the Royal Ultimate, the 6 is the 3 Virtues, the 7 is the Examination of Doubts, the 8 is the Various Verifications, and the 9 is the [5]

自南而西，自西而北，以成於一之外。七則九之自西而南者也。八則六之自北而東也。此又陰陽老少互藏其宅之變也。

洛書之縱橫十五，而七八九六，迭為消長。虛五分十，而一含九，二含八，三含七，四含六，則參伍錯綜。無適而不遇其合焉。此變化無窮之所以為妙也。

曰：然則聖人之則也，奈何？

曰：則河圖者虛其中，則洛書者總其實也。河圖之虛五與十者，太極也。奇數二十偶數二十者，兩儀也。以一二三四為六七八九者，四象也。析四方之合，以為乾坤離坎。補四隅之空，以為兌震巽艮者，八卦也。

洛書之實，其一為五行，其二為五事，其三為八政，其事為五經，其五為皇極，其六為三德，其七為稽疑，其八為庶徵，其九為福極。其位與數尤曉然矣。

I-hsüeh ch'i-meng

Happinesses and [6] Extremes.[49] Thus its positions and numbers are particularly clear.

Question: The space in the center of the Lo Text is the Supreme Polarity. The odds and evens, each totalling 20, are the Two Modes. The 1, 2, 3, and 4 containing the 9, 8, 7 and 6, and the vertical and horizontal 15's mutually formed by the 7, 8, 9 and 6 are the Four Images. The Four Cardinal Directions taken as Heaven, Earth, Fire and Water, and the four deflected corners taken as Lake, Thunder, Wind and Mountain, are the 8 Trigrams. In the River Chart, the 1 and 6 as Water, the 2 and 7 as Fire, the 3 and 8 as Wood, the 4 and 9 as Metal, and the 5 and 10 as Earth are certainly the Five Phases of the "Great Plan." And the 55 [total] are, moreover, the titles of the 9 Divisions. According to this, the Lo Text can certainly be taken as the *Changes*, and the River Chart can likewise be taken as the "Plan." So how do we know that the Chart is not the Text, and the Text is not the Chart?

Answer: Although in terms of time there is earlier and later, and although in terms of number there is greater and lesser, still in their principle (*li*) they are one and no more. In fact, the *Changes* was achieved by Fu-hsi before the Chart [appeared]. And from the first there was nothing contingent upon the Text. The Plan was obtained by the Great Yü independently from the Text; it is not necessary to trace it back to the Chart.

Moreover, by taking the River Chart and subtracting the 10, we get the Lo Text's number of 45. Subtracting the 5, we get the number of the Great Amplification, 50.[50] Adding 5 and 10 we get the Lo Text's vertical and horizontal number, 15. Taking 5 and multiplying it by 10, or 10 multiplied by 5, we again get, in both cases, the number of the Great

曰：洛書而虛其中，則亦太極也。奇偶各居二十，則亦兩儀也。一二三四而含九八七六，縱橫十五而互為七八九六，則亦四象也。四方之正，以為乾坤離坎。四隅之偏，以為兌震巽艮，則亦八卦也。河圖之一六為水，二七為火，三八為木，四九為金，五十為土，則固洪範之五行。而五十有五者，又九疇之子目也。是則洛書固可以為易，而河圖亦可以為範矣。且又安知圖之不為書。書之不為圖也邪。

曰：是其時雖有先後，數雖有多寡，然其為理則一而已。但易乃伏羲之所先得乎圖，而初無所待於書。範則大禹之所得乎書，而未必追考於圖耳。

且以河圖而虛十，則洛書四十有五之。虛五則大衍五十之數也。積五與十，則洛書縱橫十五之數也。以五乘十，以十乘五，則

Amplification. The Lo Text's 5 itself contains 5 and yields 10, and so completely constitutes the number of the Great Amplification. Adding 5 and 10 it then yields 15, completely constituting the number of the River Chart.

If we understand it like this, then we unite the crooked and straight, with nothing that is not included. So in the River Chart and the Lo Text, how can there be a distinction between first and last, or this and that?

又皆大衍之數也。洛書之五，又自含五而得十，而通為大衍之數矣。積五與十，則得十五，而通為河圖之數矣。

苟明乎此，則橫斜曲直，無所不通。而河圖洛書，又豈有先後彼此之間哉。

II. The Original Drawing of the Trigrams[51]

In ancient times, when Pao-hsi [i.e., Fu-hsi] ruled the world, he looked up and contemplated the images in heaven; he looked down and contemplated the patterns on earth. He contemplated the markings of the birds and beasts and their adaptations to the various regions. From near at hand he abstracted images from his own body; from afar he abstracted from things. In this way he first created the Eight Trigrams, to spread the power of [his] spiritual clarity (*shen-ming*) and to classify the dispositions of the myriad things.[52]

In Change there is the Supreme Polarity (*t'ai-chi*). This gives rise to the Two Modes; the Two Modes give rise to the Four Images; the Four Images give rise to the Eight Trigrams.[53]

This is how the Great Treatise describes what Pao-hsi took from in drawing the Trigrams. Thus the *I* was not made simply from the River Chart. For within Heaven and Earth there is nothing that is not the wonder of *t'ai-chi* and *yin-yang*. It was to this that the Sage looked up in contemplation and looked down in examination, seeking from afar and taking from the near at hand. Of course, he could register things in his mind silently and transcendentally [i.e. seeing things not immediately apparent].

Thus before the Two Modes are divided, the Principle of the Two Modes and Four Images and Sixty-four Hexagrams is already clear in the undifferentiated Supreme Polarity. When the Supreme Polarity divides into the Two Modes, the Supreme Polarity is certainly still Supreme Polarity, and the

原卦畫第二

古者包犧氏之王天下也，仰則觀象於天，俯則觀法於地。觀鳥獸之文與地之宜，近取諸身，遠取諸物。於是始作八卦，以通神明之德，以類萬物之情。

易有太極，是生兩儀。兩儀生四象，四象生八卦。

大傳又言包犧畫卦所取如此。則易非獨以河圖而作也。蓋盈天地之間，莫非太極陰陽之妙。聖人於此仰觀俯察，遠求近取，固有以超然而默契於其心矣。

故自以兩儀之未分也，渾然太極，而兩儀四象六十四卦之理，已粲然於其中。自太極而分兩儀，則太極固太極也，兩儀固兩儀也

Two Modes are certainly still the Two Modes. When the Two Modes divide into the Four Images, the Two Modes are still the Supreme Polarity, and the Four Images are still the Two Modes. From this it extends from 4 to 8, 8 to 16, 16 to 32, 32 to 64, and thus to 100, 1,000, 10,000 and 100,000 without end. Although their manifestation in the patterned drawings seems as if they came in temporal order from human activity, nevertheless the forms already determined and the tendencies already complete were certainly already complete in the midst of the undifferentiated chaos; there was not the slightest bit of mental activity in it. What Master Ch'eng [Hao] said about the method of multiplication can be said to "sum it up in a word."[54] What Master Shao [Yung] said about there being [the system of] Change before it was drawn is truly not mistaken.

Some current scholars have not examined this. Often they think the Sage created the *I* simply by exhausting his mind in searching for it, and obtaining it cleverly. Those who take this to the extent of saying that the drawing of the hexagrams must have been based on the milfoil [i.e., that the hexagram lines are representations of milfoil stalks] are making an even more serious mistake.

Figure 3

In Change there is the Supreme Polarity.

"Supreme Polarity" refers to the unformed state of the images and numbers, with their principles already complete in it. Forms and vessels are already complete in it, yet their principles are without visible sign. In both the River Chart and the Lo Text it is the image of the empty center. Master Chou [Tun-i], in saying "Non-Polar, and yet Supreme

。自兩儀而分四象，則兩儀又為太極，而四象又為兩儀矣。自是而推之，由四而八，由八而十六，由十六而三十二，由三十二而六十四，以至於百千萬億之無窮。雖其見於摹畫者若有先後而出於人為，然其已定之形，已成之勢，則固已具於渾然之中，而不容毫髮思慮作為於其閒也。程子所謂加一倍法者，可謂一言以蔽之。而邵子所謂畫前有易者，又可見其真不妄矣。

世儒於此，或不之察。往往以為聖人作易蓋極其心思探索之巧而得之。甚者至謂凡卦之畫，必由蓍而後得；其誤益以甚矣。

圖注三

易有太極

太極者，象數未形，而其理已具之稱。形器已具，而其理無眹之目。在河圖洛書，皆虛中之象也。周子曰：無極而太極。邵子曰

I-hsüeh ch'i-meng

Polarity!"[55] and Master Shao [Yung], in saying "The Tao is the Supreme Polarity"[56] and also "The mind is the Supreme Polarity,"[57] were speaking of this.

Figure 4

This generates the Two Modes.

The Supreme Polarity's division first generates one odd [undivided] line and one even [divided] line, making two single-line diagrams. These are the Two Modes. Their numbers, then, are *yang*: 1 and *yin*: 2. In the River Chart and the Lo Text, these are the odd and even [numbers]. Master Chou said, "The Supreme Polarity in activity generates *yang*; yet at the limit of activity it is still. In stillness it generates *yin*; yet at the limit of stillness it is also active. Activity and stillness alternate; each is the basis of the other. In distinguishing *yin* and *yang*, the Two Modes are thereby established."[58] Master Shao said, "The 1 divides into 2."[59] Both were speaking of this.

Figure 5

The Two Modes generate the Four Images.

From the Two Modes, each generates one more odd and one more even line, making four two-line diagrams. These are called the Four Images. Their positions are Mature *Yang*, 1; Young *Yin*, 2; Young *Yang*, 3; Mature *Yin*, 4. Their numbers are Mature *Yang*, 9; Young *Yin*, 8; Young *Yang*, 7; Mature *Yin*, 6. Speaking of them in terms of the River Chart, the 6 is obtained from 1 and 5; 7 is obtained from 2 and 5; 8 is obtained from 3 and 5; 9 is obtained from 4 and 5. Speaking of them in terms of the Lo Text, 9 is the difference of 1 and 10; 8 is the difference of 2 and 10; 7 is the difference

：道為太極。又曰：心為太極。此之謂也。

圖注四

是生兩議

太極之判，始生一奇一耦，而為一畫者二，是為兩議。其數則陽一而陰二。在河圖洛書，則奇耦是也。周之所謂太極動而生陽。動極而靜，靜而生陰。靜極復動。一動一靜，互為其根。分陰分陽，兩儀立焉。邵子所謂一分為二者皆謂此也。

圖注五

兩儀生四象

兩儀之上，各生一奇一耦，而為二畫者四。是謂四象。其位則太陽一，少陰二，少陽三，太陰四。其數則太陽九，少陰八，少陽七，太陰六。以河圖言之，則六者一而得於五者也，七者二而得於五者也，八者三而得於五者也，九者四而得於五者也。以洛書言之，則九者

of 3 and 10; and 6 is the difference of 4 and 10. What Master Chou said about water, fire, wood, and metal;[60] and what Master Shao said about the 2 dividing into 4,[61] both referred to this.

Figure 6

The Four Images generate the Eight Trigrams.

From the Four Images, each generates one more odd and one more even line, making eight three-line diagrams. In these are contained in outline the Three Powers,[62] as well as the names of the Eight Trigrams. Their positions are Ch'ien, 1; Tui, 2; Li, 3; Chen, 4; Sun, 5; K'an, 6; Ken, 7; and K'un, 8. In the River Chart, Ch'ien, K'un, Li and K'an occupy the four filled [places, i.e. the four cardinal directions], while Tui, Chen, Sun and Ken separately occupy the four empty [places, i.e. the four corners; see above, p. 12]. In the Lo Text, Ch'ien, K'un, Li and K'an separately occupy the Four Directions, and Tui, Chen, Sun and Ken separately occupy the four corners [see above, p. 13]. This is what the *Rituals of Chou* means by "The three *Change* [...] Classics all have eight trigrams;"[63] what the "Great Treatise" means by "The Eight Trigrams achieve their arrangement;"[64] and what Master Shao meant by "The 4 divide into 8."[65] They all were speaking in reference to this.

Figure 7

From the Eight Trigrams each generates one odd and one even line, making sixteen four-line diagrams, which do not appear in the Classic. This is what Master Shao meant by "The Eight divide into Sixteen."[66] They can also be made by

十分一之餘也,八者十分二之餘也,七者十分三之餘也,六者十分四之餘也。周子所謂水火木金,邵子所謂二分為四者皆謂此也。

圖注六

四象生八卦

四象之上,各生一奇一耦,而為三畫者八。於是三才略具,而有八卦之名矣。其位則乾一兌二離三震四巽五坎六艮七坤八。在河圖,則乾坤離坎分居四實,兌震巽艮分居四虛。在洛書,則乾坤離坎分居四方,兌震巽艮分居四隅。《周禮》所謂三易經卦皆八,《大傳》所謂八卦成列。邵子所謂四分為八者,皆指此而言也。

圖注七

八卦之上,各生一奇一耦而為四畫者十六,於經無見。邵子所謂八分為十六者是也。又為兩儀之上,各加八卦,又為八卦之上,各加兩儀也。

adding the Eight Trigrams to each of the Two Modes, or by adding the Two Modes to the Eight Trigrams.

Figure 8

On each of the four-line diagrams is generated one odd and one even line, making thirty-two five-line diagrams. This is what Master Shao meant by "The 16 divide into 32."[67] They can also be made by adding the Eight Trigrams to each of the Four Images, or by adding the Four Images to the Eight Trigrams.

Figure 9

On each of the five-line diagrams is generated one odd and one even line, making sixty-four six-line diagrams, thus joining the Three Powers and doubling them. Adding the Eight Trigrams to each of the Eight Trigrams also completes them. From these are established the names of the Sixty-four Hexagrams, and the Way of Change is grandly completed. This is what the *Rituals of Chou* means by "the three *Change* [Classics] all have sixty-four parts;"[68] what the "Great Treatise" means by "thereupon they are multiplied and the lines are contained within;"[69] and what Master Shao meant by "the 32 divide into 64."[70]

Similarly, we can take each hexagram and again on each generate one odd and one even line, making 128 seven-line diagrams; and again on each seven-line diagram generate one odd and one even, making 256 eight-line diagrams; and on each eight-line diagram generate one odd and one even line, making 512 nine-line diagrams; and again on each of the nine-line diagrams generate one odd and one even line, making 1,024 ten-line diagrams; and on each of the ten-line diagrams

圖注八

四畫之上，各生一奇一耦，而為五畫者三十二。邵子所謂十六分為三十二者是也。又為四象之上，各加八卦。又為八卦之上，各加四象也。

圖注九

五畫之上，各生一奇一耦，而為六畫者六十四，則兼三才而兩之。而八卦之乘八卦亦周。於是六十四卦之名立而易道大成矣。《周禮》所謂"三易之別皆六十有四。《大傳》所謂"因而重之爻在其中矣。邵子所謂"三十二分為六十"四者是也。

若於其上各卦，又各生一奇一耦，則為七畫者百二十八矣。七畫之上又各生一奇一耦，則為八畫者二百五十六矣。八畫之上又各生一奇一耦，則為九畫者五百十二矣。九畫之上又各生一奇一耦，則為十畫者千二十四

generate one odd and one even line, making 2,048 eleven-line diagrams; and on each of the eleven-line diagrams generate one odd and one even, making 4,096 twelve-line diagrams. This is the number of changing hexagrams of Chiao Kan's *I Lin* (Grove of Changes), multiplying the 64 by 64.[71]

I will not now duplicate a chart of this, as its outline can be seen in the fourth chapter. If from the 12-line diagrams we continue generating odd and even lines, eventually we come to 24-line diagrams, for a total of 16,777,216 changes. Taking 4,096 and multiplying it by itself also gives this sum. Expanding this we do not know where it ultimately ends. Although we cannot see its usefulness, it is sufficient to show that the Way of Change is indeed inexhaustible.

Figures 10 & 11

Heaven and Earth determine the positions. Mountain and Lake interpenetrate their *ch'i*. Thunder and Wind arouse each other. Water and Fire do not combat each other. Thus the Eight Trigrams are intermingled.

One who calculates the past goes with [the movement of Heaven]. One who knows the future goes against [the movement of Heaven]. Thus the *I* has reverse calculations (*ni-shu*)[72]

Thunder serves to move things; Wind to scatter them; Rain to moisten them; Sun to warm them; Ken (Mountain) to stop them; Tui (Lake) to please them; Ch'ien (Heaven) to lord over them; K'un (Earth) to store them.[73]

矣。十畫之上，又各生一奇一耦，則為十一畫者二千四十八矣。十一畫之上又各生一奇一耦，則為十二畫者四千九十六矣。此焦贛易林變卦之數，蓋亦六十四乘六十四也。

今不復為圖於此，而略是第四篇中。若自十二畫上，又各生一奇一耦，累至二十四，則成千六百七十七萬七千二百一十六變。以四千九十六自相乘，其數亦與此和。引而伸之，蓋未知其所終極也。雖未見其用處，然亦足以見易道之無窮矣。

圖注十，十一

天地定位，山澤通氣，雷風相薄，水火不相射，八卦相錯。

數往者順，知來者逆。是故易，逆數也。

雷以動之，風以散之，雨以潤之，日以晅之，艮以止之，兌以說之，乾以君之，坤以藏之。

I-hsüeh ch'i-meng

Master Shao said:

This section explains the Eight Trigrams of Fu-hsi (Fig. 10). The alternations of the Eight Trigrams illuminate their interactions and complete the Sixty-four (Fig. 11). "One who calculates the past goes with" is like movement in accordance with Heaven.[74] This is a movement to the left [counter-clockwise], in each step toward the previously-generated trigram [in terms of the seasons]. Thus it is called "calculating the past." "One who knows the future goes against" is like movement opposite to Heaven. This is a movement to the right, in each step toward the not-yet-generated trigrams. Thus it is called "knowing the future," and the calculations of the *I* are completed by going against [the rotation of Heaven]. This section directly explains the ideas of [Fu-hsi's] chart in terms of reverse [anticipatory] knowledge of the Four Seasons.[75]

[Ts'ai Yüan-ting:] Examining it in terms of the horizontal diagram (Fig. 6), there is Ch'ien in the first position and Tui in the second; with Tui in the second there is Li in the third with Li in the third there is Chen in the fourth; with Chen in the fourth there is Sun in the fifth, K'an in the sixth, Ken in the seventh, and K'un in the eighth, also generated in sequence. This is how the *I* was completed.

On the left side of the circular chart (Fig. 10), from the beginning of Chen as winter up to the middle of Li and Tui as the spring equinox, and extending to the end of Ch'ien, where the summer solstice is encountered [i.e. clockwise], each step yields the previously-generated trigram [in terms

邵子曰：

"此一節，明伏羲八卦也。八卦相錯者，明交相錯，而成六十四也。數往者順若順天而行。是左旋也，皆已生之卦也。故云‧數往也。，知來者順。‧若逆天而行。是右行也，皆未生之卦也。故云‧知來也，。夫易之數，由逆而成矣。此一節，直解圖意，若逆知四時之 謂也。

〔蔡元定〕以橫圖觀之，有乾一而後有兌二，有兌二而後有離三，有離三而後有震四，有震四而巽五坎六艮七坤八，亦以次而生焉。此易之所以成也。

而圓圖之左方，自震之初為冬至，離兌之中為春分，以至於之乾之末而交

of their numbers in Fig. 6], like calculating yesterday from today. Thus it says, "One who calculates the past goes with [the normal seasonal progression]."

On the right side, from the beginning of Sun as the summer solstice to the middle of K'an and Ken as the autumn equinox, and extending to the end of K'un where the winter solstice is encountered [also clockwise], each step yields the not-yet-generated trigram [in terms of both the numbers and the seasons]. like anticipating tomorrow from today. Thus it says, "One who knows the future goes against [the normal, counter-clockwise rotation of Heaven]."

In this way the original *I* was completed progressively from beginning to end, like the sequence of the horizontal chart and the right side of the circular chart. Thus it says, "The *I* has reverse calculations.[76]

[Shao] further said:

Once the Supreme Polarity divides, the Two Modes are established. The *yang* rises to interact with the *yin*, and the *yin* descends to interact with the *yang*, and the Four Images are generated. *Yang* interacts with *yin*, and *yin* interacts with *yang* to generate the Four Images of Heaven. The firm interacts with the yielding, and yielding interacts with the firm to generate the Four Images of Earth.... The Eight Trigrams alternate with each other, and then are the Myriad Things born. Therefore, 1 divides into 2, 2 divides into 4, 4 divides into 8, 8 divides into 16, 16 divides into 32, and 32 divides into 64.... It is like the root with its trunk, and the trunk with its branches. The bigger it is, the fewer; the finer it is, the more numerous. Therefore,

夏至焉，皆進而得其已生之卦。猶自今日而追數昨日也。故曰"數往者順"其右方，

自巽之初為夏至，坎艮之中為秋分，以至於坤之末而交冬至焉，皆進而得其未生之卦。猶自今日而逆計來日也。故曰"知來者逆"。

然本易之所以成，則其先後始終如橫圖及圓圖右方之序而已。故曰"易，逆數也"。

又曰：

太極既分，兩儀立矣。陽上交於陰，陰下交於陽，而四象生矣。陽交於陰，陰交於陽，而生天之四象。剛交於柔，柔交於剛，而生地之四象。八卦相錯，而後萬物生焉。是故一分為二，二分為四，四分為八，八分為十六，十六分為三十二，三十二分為六十四

Ch'ien serves to divide things, K'un to assemble them; Chen to enlarge them, Sun to diminish them. Enlarged, they divide; divided, they are diminished; diminished, they contract.[77]

Ch'ien and K'un determine the positions; Chen and Sun are the first mixing [of *yang* and *yin*]; Tui, Li, K'an and Ken are the second mixing. Thus in Chen the *yang* lines are few and the *yin* are greater in number. In Sun the *yin* are few and the *yang* are greater in number. In Tui and Li the *yang* have progressively become greater. In K'an and Ken the *yin* have gradually become greater.[78]

He [Shao] further said:

Before the Non-polar (*wu-chi*), *yin* contains *yang*.[79] After there are images [in a perceptibly differentiated state], *yang* divides into *yin*. *Yin* is *yang*'s mother; *yang* is *yin*'s father. Thus the mother is pregnant with the eldest son, making Fu [Hexagram 24, Return]. The father gives rise to the eldest daughter, making Kou [Hexagram 44, Encounter). This is how *yang* arises in Fu and *yin* arises in Kou.[80]

He [Shao] further said:

As Chen begins to adulturate its *yin*, *yang* is generated. As Sun begins to decrease its *yang*, *yin* is generated. Tui's *yang* is mature, and Ken's *yin* is mature. Chen and Tui are included in the *yin* of Heaven. Sun and Ken are included in the *yang* of Earth. This is because Chen and Tui have *yin* above and *yang* below, and Sun and Ken have *yang* above *yin* below. When we say that Heaven begins to generate, it is because the *yin* is above and the *yang* is below. Their interaction is the meaning of T'ai [Peace, hexagram 11]. When we speak of Earth having reached completion, it is because the *yang* is above and *yin* is below [in hexagram 12, P'i, Standstill] in the positions of honor and submission.[81]

。猶根之有幹，幹之有枝。愈大則愈小，愈細則愈繁。

是故乾以分之，坤以翕之，震以長之，巽以消之。長則分，分則消，消則翕也。乾坤定位也，震巽一交也，兌離坎艮再交也。故震陽少而陰尚多也；巽陰少而陽尚多也；兌離陽浸多也，坎艮陰浸多也。

又曰：

無極之前，陰含陽也。有象之後，陽分陰也。陰為陽之母，陽為陰之父。故母孕長男而為復，父生長女而為姤。是以陽起於復，陰起於姤也。

又曰：

"震始交陰而陽生。巽始消陽而陰生。兌，陽長也，艮，陰長也。震兌，在天之陰也。巽艮，在地之陽也。故震兌上陰而下陽，巽艮上陽而下陰。天以始生言之，故陰上而陽下，交秦之議也。地以既成言之，故陽上而陰下。

I-hsüeh ch'i-meng

Ch'ien and K'un determine the upper and lower positions. K'an and Li arrange the gates, left and right. In the opening and closing of Heaven and Earth; in the coming and going of the sun and moon; in spring, summer, fall and winter; the old moon, new moon, quarter moon, and full moon; day and night; growth and decline; action and measure; fullness and deficiency; there is nothing that does not follow from this.[82]

> [Ts'ai Yüan-ting:] "As Chen begins to alternate its *yin*, *yang* is generated" refers to the circular chart (Fig. 10), in which Chen and K'un are adjacent and one *yang* is generated [to change from K'un to Chen]. "As Sun begins to decrease its *yang*, *yin* is generated" also refers to the circular chart, in which Sun and Ch'ien are adjacent and one *yin* is generated [to change from Ch'ien to Sun].

[Shao] also said:

If we consider the 48 of Ch'ien [i.e. the total of 48 lines in all the hexagrams with Ch'ien at the bottom] in four divisions, one division [¼] consists in those that have been overcome by *yin* [i.e. the 12 *yin* lines]. If we consider the 48 of K'un in four divisions, one division consists in the *yang* that has been overcome [i.e. the 12 *yang* lines "missing" from the 48 of Ch'ien]. Thus Ch'ien gets 36 and K'un gets 12.[83]

> [Ts'ai Yüan-ting:] Further thought on Tui and Li, etc.: We take Tui and Li to have 28 *yang* and 20 *yin*. Chen has 20 *yang* and 28 *yin*. Ken and K'an have 28 *yin* and 20 *yang*. Sun has 20 *yin* and 28 *yang*.

[Shao] further said:

乾坤定之位也，尊卑上下之位，坎離列左右之門。天地之所闔闢，日月之所出入，春夏秋冬。晦朔弦望，晝夜長短，行度盈縮，莫不由乎此矣"。

〔蔡元定〕"震始交陰而陽生"，是說圓圖震與坤接一陽生也。"巽始消陽而陰生"，是說圓圖巽與乾接而一陰生也。

又曰：

乾四十八而四分之，一分為陰所剋也。坤四十八而四分之，一分為所剋之陽也。故乾得三十六，而坤得十二也。"兌離以下更思之。

今按：兌離二十八陽，二十陰；震二十陽，二十陰；艮坎二十八陰，二十陽；巽二十陰，二十八陽。

又曰，

I-hsüeh ch'i-meng

Ch'ien and K'un [arranged] vertically and their six children horizontally [i.e. in the Fu-hsi sequence] is the basis of the *I*.[84]

And:

When *yang* is inside *yin*, the *yang* moves backwards. When *yin* is inside *yang*, the *yin* moves backwards. *Yang* inside *yang* and *yin* inside *yin* both move forward. This is the principle of complete perfection. In the tables and charts it is indeed apparent.[85]

And:

From Fu to Ch'ien [left half of Fu-hsi's Chart of the Sixty-four Hexagrams, Fig. 11] there are, altogether, 112 *yang* lines. From Kou to K'un [right half] there are altogether 80 *yang* lines. From Kou to K'un there are altogether 112 *yin* lines. From Fu to Ch'ien there are altogether 80 *yin* lines.[86]

And:

K'an and Li are the limits of *yin* and *yang*. Therefore Li corresponds to *yin* [the 3rd "branch"of the sixty-year calendar, corresponding to East-Northeast] and K'an corresponds to *shen* [the 9th branch; West-Southwest]; their numbers' regular excess is the overflow of *yin* and *yang*. However, the functional numbers do not exceed the mean.

> [Ts'ai Yüan-ting:] This deserves further thought. Li [contrary to what Shao says] corresponds to *mao* [4th branch; East] and K'an corresponds to

乾坤從而六子橫,易之本也。

又曰,

陽在陰中,陽逆行。陰在陽中,陰逆行。陽在陽中,陰在陰中,則皆順行。此真至之理,桉圖可見之矣。

又曰:

復至乾,凡百一十有二陽。姤至姤坤,凡八十陽。姤至坤凡百一十有二陰。復至乾凡八十陰。

又曰:

坎離者,陰陽之限也。故離常酉,坎常申。而數常踰之者,陰陽之溢也。然用數不過乎中也。

〔蔡元定〕此更宜思。離當卯,坎當酉。但以坤為子半可見矣。

West. Simply by taking K'un as *tzu* [1st branch; North] in the middle, it can be seen.

[Shao] also said:

A priori (*hsien-t'ien*, Before Heaven) studies are the method of the mind/heart (*hsin-fa*). Therefore the charts always are generated from the center (*chung*), and the myriad transformations and the myriad events are generated in the mind/heart (*hsin*).[87]

And:

Although the charts have no text, one can discuss them all day and never leave the subject. This is because the principles of Heaven and Earth and the myriad things are completely manifested in them.[88]

Figure 12

The Lord (*Ti*) comes forth in Chen; he regulates in Sun, causes mutual perception in Li, brings about service in K'un, joyful words in Tui, battle in Ch'ien, toil in K'an, and fulfilled words in Ken.

The myriad things come forth in Chen; Chen is in the East. They are regulated in Sun; Sun is in the Southeast. "Regulation" means the purity and perfection of the myriad things. Li is brightness, and the mutual perception of all the myriad things. It is the trigram of the South. The Sage faces South and hears the whole world, ruling while facing the light; this [practice] is taken from this [idea]. K'un is Earth; all the myriad things are nourished in it. Thus we say "brings about service in K'un." Tui is the beginning of autumn, which is what pleases the

又曰：

先天學心法也，故圖皆自中起。萬化萬事生於心也。

又曰：

圖雖無文，吾終日言而未嘗離乎是。天地萬物之理盡在其中矣"。

圖注十二

帝出乎震；齊乎巽，相見乎離，致役乎坤，說言乎兌，戰乎乾，勞乎坎，成言乎艮。

萬物出乎震，震東方也。齊乎巽，巽東南也。齊也者，言萬物之潔齊也。離也者，明也。萬物皆相見，南方之卦也。聖人南面而聽天下，嚮明而治，蓋取諸也。坤也者，地也。萬物皆致養焉，故曰"致役乎坤"。兌，

myriad things. Thus we say "joyful words in Tui." "Doing battle in Ch'ien" is Ch'ien, the trigram of the Northwest. This refers to the *yin* and *yang* displacing each other. K'an is water, and is the trigram of true North, the trigram of toil. It is what the myriad things return to -- thus it says "toil in K'an." Ken is the trigram of the Northeast. It is what fulfills the end and fulfills the beginning of the myriad things. Thus we say "fulfilled words in Ken."[89]

Spirit (*shen*) is what is referred to by the "wondrous" myriad things. In animating the myriad things, nothing is more forceful than thunder. In scattering the myriad things, nothing is more effective than wind. In drying the myriad things, nothing is more parching than fire. In pleasing the myriad things, nothing pleases like a lake. In moistening the myriad things, nothing moistens like water. In ending the myriad things and beginning the myriad things, nothing succeeds like Ken. Thus water and fire approach each other, thunder and wind do not oppose each other, mountain and lake mingle their *ch'i*. Only then can there be change and transformation, which fulfills the myriad things.[90]

Master Shao said:

This section clarifies the Eight Trigrams of King Wen (Fig. 12).

He also said:

Perfect indeed was King Wen's creation of the *I*. He grasped the functioning of Heaven and Earth. Thus Ch'ien and K'un interact to make T'ai [Hexagram 11, Peace] and K'an and Li combine to make Chi-ch'i [Hexagram 63, After Completion]. Ch'ien arises in *tzu* [1st

正秋也，萬物之所說也。故曰"說言乎兌"。戰乎乾。乾，西北之卦也，言陰陽相薄也。坎者，水也，正北方之卦也，勞卦，萬物之所歸也，故曰"勞乎坎"。艮，東北之卦也，萬物之所成終而所成始也，故曰"成言乎艮。

神也者，妙萬物而為言者也。動萬物者莫疾乎雷。撓萬物者莫疾乎風，。燥萬物者莫熯乎火。說萬物者莫說乎澤。潤萬物者莫潤乎水。終萬物始萬物者莫盛乎艮。故水火相逮，雷風不相悖，山澤通氣。然後能變化既成萬物也。

邵子曰：

此一節明文王八卦也"。

又曰：

至哉，文王之作易也。其得天地之用乎。故乾坤交而為泰，坎離交而為既濟也。乾生於

branch: midnight, North], K'un arises in *wu* [7th branch: noon, South]; K'un ends in *yin* [3rd branch: 4 a.m., East-Northeast], Li ends in *shen* [9th branch: 4 p.m., West-Southwest]; they thereby [cor]respond to the seasons of Heaven [time]. Placing Ch'ien in the Northwest and relegating K'un to the Southwest, then the eldest son [Chen] performs service [in the East], and the eldest daughter [Sun] substitutes for the mother [in the Southeast]. K'an [North] and Li [South] take their positions, and Tui [West] and Ken [Northeast] are paired, thereby [cor]responding to the directions [domains] of Earth [space]. A model of kingship [Ts'ai Yüan-ting adds: was King Wen]. He epitomized it in this.[91]

> [Ts'ai Yüan-ting:] This speaks of King Wen modifying the intention [meaning] of Fu-hsi's trigram chart.[92] Thus from the combining of Ch'ien in the South and K'un in the North, and then [reversing them] Ch'ien in the North and K'un in the South, we make T'ai [Peace]. From the combining of Li in the East and K'an in the West, and then Li in the West and K'an in the East, we make Chi-ch'i [After Completion, Hexagram 63]. The combination of Ch'ien and K'un comes from their completion and their reversion to where they came from.

Thus, with a second change, Ch'ien retreats to the Northwest and K'un retreats to the Southwest [changing Fu-hsi's diagram to King Wen's]. The alterations of K'an and Li are: from the East, upwards and westward [Li], and from the West, downward and eastward [K'an]. Therefore, once Ch'ien and K'un retire, Li gets Ch'ien's position and K'an gets K'un's position. Chen's performing service appears on the East side and Sun's

子，坤生於午，坎終於寅離終於申，以應天之時也。置乾於西北，退坤於西南。長子用事，而長女代母。坎離得位，而兌艮為耦，以應地之方也。王者之法，交王也。其盡於是矣"。

〔蔡元定〕此言文王改易伏羲卦圖之意也。蓋自乾南坤北而交，則乾北坤南而為泰矣。自離東坎西而交，則離西坎東而為既濟矣。乾坤之交者，自其所已成，而反其所由生也。

故再變則乾退乎西北，坤退乎西南也。坎離之變者，東自上而西，西自下而東也。故乾坤既退，則離得乾位而坎得坤位也。震用事者發生於東方，巽代母者，長鄰於東南也。

又曰：

I-hsüeh ch'i-meng

substituting for the mother grows and nourishes in the Southeast.

[Shao] also said:

"Change" (*i*) is what is meant by "the alternation of *yin* and *yang*."[93] Chen and Tui begin the interaction; therefore they are placed in the positions of morning and evening. Ken and Li interact to the utmost; therefore they are placed in the positions of midnight and noon. Sun and Ken do not interact, but their *yin* and *yang* is still mixed; therefore they are placed on the side among the functioning [trigrams]. Ch'ien and K'un are pure *yang* and pure *yin*, and so are placed in non-functioning positions.[94]

He also said:

Tui, Li and Sun get the majority of *yang* [lines]; Ken, K'an and Chen get the majority of *yin*. For this reason they constitute the functioning of Heaven and Earth. Ch'ien is completely *yang*, and K'un is completely *yin*. Therefore they do not function.[95]

He also said:

Chen and Tui horizontally and the Six Trigrams vertically [i.e., the King Wen sequence] are the functioning of the *I*.[96]

> [Ts'ai Yüan-ting:] Having examined this chart, I would explain it further. As for Chen in the East and Tui in the West: *Yang* chiefly progresses, so we take the elder as prior and place him on the left. *Yin* chiefly retires, so we take the younger as honored and place her on the right. As for K'an in the North: it is in the process of progressing. Li in the South is in the process of retreating. The

易者一陰一陽之謂也。震兌始交者也,故常朝夕之位。坎離交之極者也,故常子午之位。巽艮不交而陰陽猶雜也,故當用之偏。乾坤純陽純陰也,故當不用之位也。

又曰:

兌離巽得陽之多者也;艮坎震得陰之多也,是以為天地用也。乾極陽,坤極陰,是以不用也。

又曰:

震兌 橫而六 卦縱易之用也。

〔蔡元定〕嘗考此圖而更為之說曰:震東兌西者,陽主進,故以長為先而位乎左。陰主退,故以少為貴而位乎右也。坎北者,進之中也。離南者,退之中也。男北而女南者,互藏其宅也。四者皆當四方之正位,而為用事之卦。然震兌始而坎離終,震兌輕而坎離重也。

male in the North and the female in the South shelter each other's domiciles. These four are all placed in the cardinal positions of the Four Directions, and are the trigrams that perform services. However, Chen and Tui initiate, and K'an and Li complete. Chen and Tui are light and K'an and Li are heavy.

Ch'ien in the Northwest and K'un in the Southwest are father and mother, already old and retired, occupying non-functioning places. However, the mother is intimate and the father is noble. Therefore K'un is something like half-functioning, and Ch'ien is completely non-functioning.

Ken in the Northeast and Sun in the Southeast are the youngest male after his advancement and the oldest female before her retiring. Therefore they also are both non-functioning. However, the male has not yet been taught, and the female is about to travel [leave home to be married]. Therefore Sun has a slight tendency toward functioning, while Ken is completely non-functioning. The four all occupy the non-cardinal positions in the four corners. However, the occupants of the East [youngest son and oldest daughter] are not yet functioning, while the occupants of the West [father and mother] are no longer functioning. Therefore the text below successively brings out the six children and does not count Ch'ien and K'un. When we come to the pairing together of water and fire, thunder and wind, mountain and marsh, then we will again use Fu-hsi's version of the trigrams.

Ch'ien is strong, K'un is compliant.

乾西北坤西南者,父母既老而退居不用地也。然母親而父尊,故坤猶半用而乾全不用也。

艮東北巽東南者,少男進之後而長女退之先,故易皆不用也。然男未就傳,女將有行,故巽稍向用,而艮全未用也。四者皆居,四隅不正之位。然居東者未用而居西者不復用也。故下文歷舉六子而不數乾坤。至其水火雷風山澤之相偶,則又用伏？卦云。

**乾健也,坤順也,
震動也,巽入也,
坎陷也,離麗也,
艮止也,兌說也。**

程子曰：

> Chen is active, Sun is penetrating.
> K'an is abysmal, Li is resplendent.
> Ken is still, Tui is pleasurable.⁹⁷

Master Ch'eng [I] said:

Yang at the bottom is always an image of movement; in the middle it is an image of sinking; on top it is an image of stopping. *Yin* at the bottom is an image of penetration; in the middle is an image of resplendence; on top is an image of pleasure.

> Ch'ien is the horse, K'un is the cow.
> Chen is the dragon, Sun is the fowl.
> K'an is the pig, Li is the pheasant.
> Ken is the dog, Tui is the sheep.⁹⁸

These are the images of the various creatures "taken from afar."⁹⁹

> Ch'ien is the head, K'un is the belly.
> Chen is the feet, Sun is the thighs.
> K'an is the ears, Li is the eyes
> Ken is the hands, Tui is the mouth.¹⁰⁰

These are the images of the various parts of the body, "taken from near at hand."¹⁰¹

> Ch'ien is Heaven; therefore it is designated father. K'un is Earth; therefore it is designated mother. In Chen [she] first tries to obtain a son; therefore it is called the eldest son. In Sun [the father] first tries to obtain a daughter; therefore it is called the eldest daughter. In K'an [she] again tries to obtain a son; therefore it is called the middle son. In Li [he] again tries to obtain a daughter; therefore it is called the

凡陽在下者動之象，在中者陷之象，在上止之象。陰在下者入之象，在中者麗之象，在上說之象。

乾為馬，坤為牛，
震為龍，巽為雞，
坎為豕，離為雉，
艮為狗，兌為羊。

此遠取諸物之象。

乾為首，坤為腹，
震為足，巽為股，
坎為耳，離為目，
艮為手，兌為口。

此近取諸身之象。

乾，天也，故稱乎父。坤，地也，故稱乎母。震一索而得男，故謂之長男。巽一索而得女，故謂之長女。坎再索而得男，故謂之中男。離再索而得女，故謂之中女。艮三索而得男，故謂之少男。兌三索而得女，故謂之少女。

今桉坤求於乾，得其初九而為震，故曰"一索而得男"。乾求於坤，得其初六而為巽，故曰"一索而得女"。坤再求而得乾之九

middle daughter. In Ken [she] for the third time tries to obtain a son; therefore it is called the youngest son. In Tui [he] for the third time tries to obtain a daughter; therefore it is called the youngest daughter.[102]

In the present passage K'un seeks in Ch'ien to obtain the 9 in the first place, making Chen.[103] Thus "[The mother] first tries to obtain a son." Ch'ien seeks in K'un to obtain the 6 in the first place, making Sun. Thus "[The father] first tries to obtain a daughter." K'un again seeks to obtain a 9 from Ch'ien in the second place, thereby making K'an. Thus "[She] again tries to obtain a son." Ch'ien again seeks to obtain a 6 from K'un in the second place, thereby making Li. Thus "[He] again tries to obtain a daughter." K'un for the third time seeks to obtain a 9 from Ch'ien in the third place, thereby making Ken. Thus "[She] for the third time tries to obtain a son." Ch'ien for the third time seeks to obtain a 6 from K'un, in there third place, thereby making Tui. Thus "[He] for the third time tries to obtain a daughter."

All these sections are King Wen's observations on the already completed trigrams, extending their unexplicated images in the form of discussion. What Master Shao called "*a posteriori* studies" has to do with the functioning positions.[104]

二以為坎，故曰再"索而得男"。乾再求而得坤之六二以為離，故曰再"索而得女"。坤三求而得乾之九三以為艮，故曰三"索而得男"。乾三求而得坤之六三以為兌，故曰三"索而得女"。

凡此數節，皆文王觀於已成之卦而推其未明之象以為說。邵子所謂後天之學，入用之位者也。

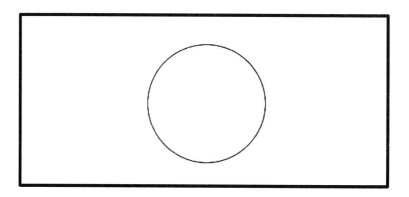

Figure 3

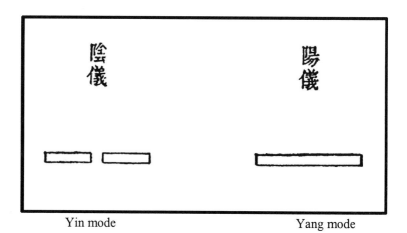

Yin mode   Yang mode

Figure 4

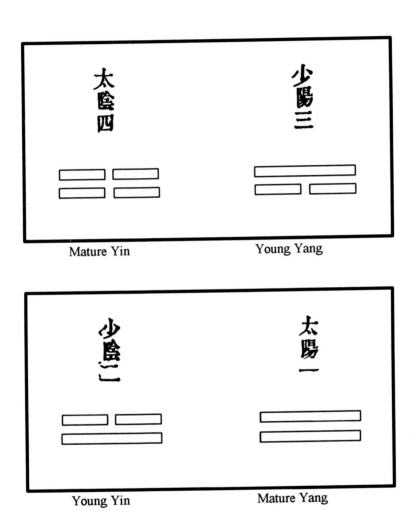

Figure 5

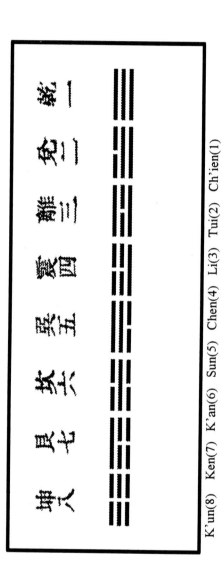

K'un(8)　Ken(7)　K'an(6)　Sun(5)　Chen(4)　Li(3)　Tui(2)　Ch'ien(1)

Figure 6

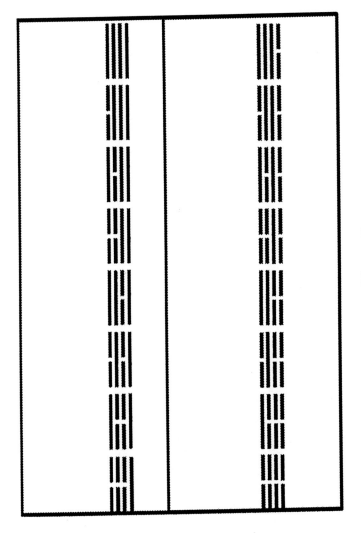

Figure 7

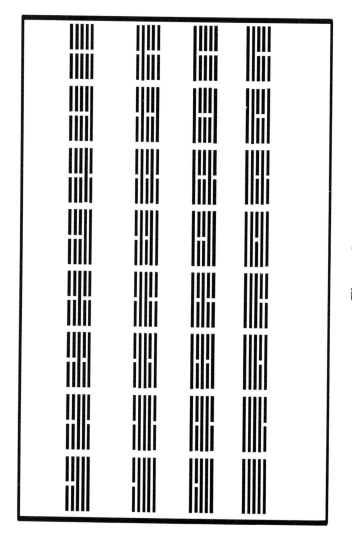

Figure 8

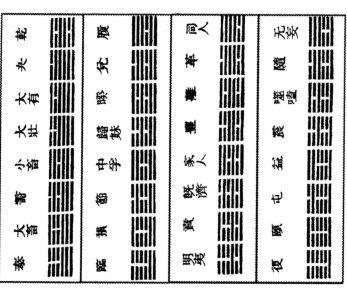

Figure 9a

Figure 9b

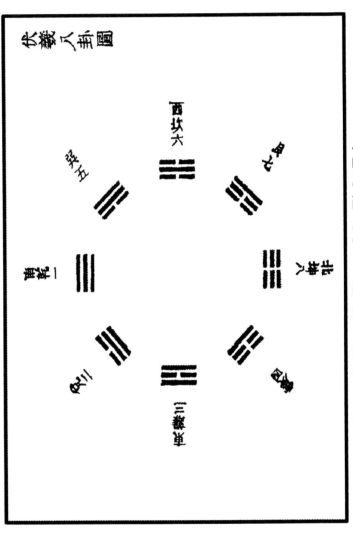

Figure 10: Fu-hsi's Chart of the Eight Trigrams

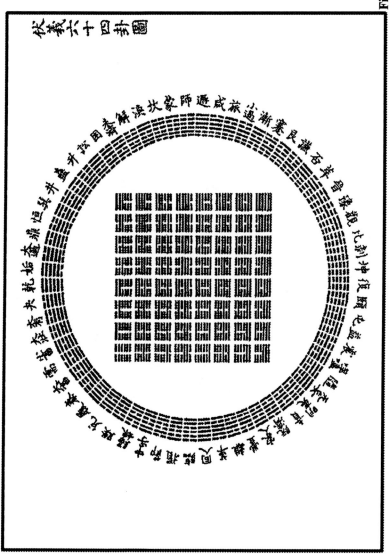

Figure 11

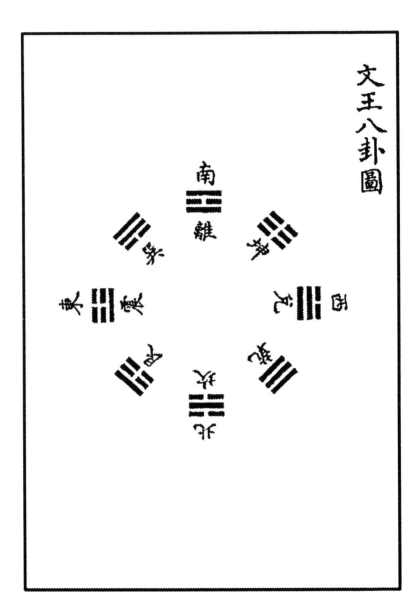

Figure 12: King Wen's Chart of the Eight Trigrams

III. Explaining the Milfoil Stalks[105]

The number of the Great Amplification is 50.[106]

The numbers in the centers of the River Chart and the Lo Text are both 5. Expanding them, each increases its number up to 10, and taking these [multiplied] together makes 50. The sum of the River Chart is 55. The 50 is always obtained from 5, and only 5 is what 50 is derived from, yet it itself is derived from nothing.[107] Thus by subtracting it we are left with 50. Also, 40 of the 55 is divided into the numbers of the mature and young *yang* and *yin*, while the 5 and 10 do nothing [i.e. are neither *yang* nor *yin*].[108] So again, by taking 5 and multiplying it by 10, or by taking 10 and multiplying it by 5, in both cases we get 50.

The sum of the Lo Text is 45, with 40 dispersed to the outside and divided into the numbers of mature and young *yin* and *yang*. Only the 5 abides in the center, doing nothing. So it also contains in itself the number 5, and altogether we get 50.

Those that are used are 49.[109]

The number of the Great Amplification is 50; the milfoil with one root and 100 stalks can correspond to twice the number of the Great Amplification. Therefore in the method of casting the milfoil, one takes 50 stalks in one hand, setting aside one unused to represent the Supreme Polarity, and so those that are actually used total 49. This is an undivided image of the embodied whole of the Two Modes.[110]

Divide them in two, to symbolize the Two [Modes]. Place one to symbolize the Three [Powers]. Count off

明蓍策第三

大衍之數五十。

河圖洛書之中數皆五。衍之而各極其數以至於十,則合為五十矣。河圖積數五十五。其五十者,皆因五而後得,獨五為五十所因,而自無所因。故虛之則但為五十。又五十五之中,其四十者分為陰陽老少之數,而其五與十者無所為。則又以五乘十,以十乘五,而亦皆為五十矣。洛書積數四十五,而其四十者,散布於外而分陰陽老少之數。

唯五居中而無所為。則亦自含五數而並為五十矣。

其用四十有九。

大衍之數五十,而蓍一根百莖,付當大衍之數者二。故揲蓍之法,取五十莖為一握,置其一不用,以象太極,而其當用之策,凡四十有九。蓋兩儀體具而未分之象也。

分而為二以象兩,掛一以象三,揲之以四,以象四時,歸奇於扐以象閏。五歲再閏,故再扐而後掛。

I-hsüeh ch'i-meng

> by fours to symbolize the Four Seasons. Return the remainder between the fingers to represent the intercalary month. In five years there are two intercalary months; therefore place again in the next space between the fingers.[111]

"Place" means to keep between the small fingers. "Count off" means to use the thumb and index finger to separate and divide them. "The remainder" is the number [of stalks] left over. "Between the fingers" means the two spaces between the three inner fingers.

> Take all 49 milfoil stalks and randomly divide them in the middle. Hold each pile in one hand to represent the Two Modes, and place one stalk from the right hand into the space next to the little finger of the left hand, to symbolize the Three Powers. Proceed to count off by fours the stalks in the left hand to symbolize the Four Seasons, and return those left over to the space next to the fourth finger, to symbolize the intercalary month. Then count off by fours the stalks in the right hand, and again return those left over to the space next to the third finger of the left hand, to symbolize the second intercalary month in five years.

Placing the first is step one. Counting off the left-hand stalks is step two. Holding the left-hand stalks between the fingers is step three. Counting off the right-hand stalks is step four. Holding the right-hand stalks between the fingers is step five. This is called one Change (*pien*). The number of stalks placed between the fingers will be either 5 or 9.

Figure 13

The three possible arrangements of 5 are called odd.

掛者懸於小指之間。揲者以大指食指閒而別之。奇，謂餘數。扐者扐於中三指之兩閒也。

蓍凡四十有九，信手中分。各置一手，以象兩儀，而掛右手一策於左手小指之間，以象三才。逐以四揲左手之策，以象四時，而歸其餘數於左手指閒，以象閏。又以四揲右手之策，而再歸其餘數於左手第三指閒，以象在閏五歲之象。

掛左一也，揲左二也，扐左三也，揲左四也，扐右五也。是謂一變。其掛扐之數，不五即九。

圖注十三

得五者三，所謂奇也。

> [Ts'ai Yüan-ting:] "5 minus the 1 placed between the fingers is 4; taking the 4 together as 1 results in an odd number. This is the *yang* number of the Two Modes."

The single possible arrangement of 9 is called even.

> [Ts'ai Yüan-ting:] 9 minus the 1 placed between the fingers are 8; taking the 4s in 2 groups results in an even number. This is the *yin* number [2] of the Two Modes.

After the first Change, put aside those remaining [i.e. the 5 or 9 held between the fingers], and combine again the stalks still present, which may be 40 or 44. Divide, place, count off, and return them according to the former procedure. This is called the second Change. Those placed between the fingers will be either 4 or 8.

Figure 14

The two possible arrangements of 4 are called odd.

> [Ts'ai Yüan-ting:] "The 1 placed between the fingers is not discarded, and those remaining [between the fingers] are treated as in the preceding discussion [i.e., as a single unit]."

The two possible arrangements of 8 are called even.

〔蔡元定〕五除掛一既四，以四約之為一，故為奇。即兩儀之陽數也。

得九者一，所謂耦也。

〔蔡元定〕九除掛一既八，以四約之為二，故為耦。即兩儀之陰數也。

一變之後，除前餘數，復合其見存之策，或四十，或四十四。分掛揲歸如前法，是謂再變。其掛扐者，不四則八。

圖注十四

得四者一，所謂奇也。

〔蔡元定〕不去掛一，餘同前義。

得八者二，所謂耦也。

I-hsüeh ch'i-meng

> [Ts'ai Yüan-ting:] "The 1 placed between the fingers is not discarded, and those remaining [between the fingers] are treated as in the preceding discussion [i.e., as two groups of 4]."

After the second Change, put aside those remaining [between the fingers], and combine again the present stalks, which may be 40, 36, or 32. Divide, place, count off and return them according to the former procedure. This is called the third Change. Those placed between the fingers will be the same as those in the second Change [i.e. 4 or 8].

When the three Changes are completed, combine them and observe the odd and even numbers of those placed between the fingers, in order to distinguish the mature and young *yin* and *yang* that have come about. This is considered one line.

Figure 15

Above (Fig. 15) are all twelve cases of three odds making the mature *yang* [9]. The number of stalks placed between the fingers is 13; subtracting the single 1 makes 12. Dividing 4 by 3 yields three 1s. A 1 represents a circle with a circumference of 3. Thus among the three 1s each contains 3, so the total sum of three 3s is 9. The number that has been counted off is 36 [49 - 13]; grouping this by fours also yields 9.

> [Ts'ai Yüan-ting:] Subtracting 1 from those placed between the fingers [13] yields the same as dividing 48 by 4. This one 12, or 3 times 4, is the mother of 9. The number of stalks counted off [36] is 3 times what is gotten by dividing 48 by 4. Tripling the 12, or multiplying 4 by 9, yields the

〔蔡元定〕不去掛一，餘同前義。

再變之後，除前兩次餘數，復合其見存之策，或四十，或三十六，或三十二。分掛揲歸如前法，是謂三變。其掛扐者，如再變例。

三變既畢，乃合三變，視其掛扐奇耦，以分所遇陰之老少。是謂一爻。

圖注十五

右三奇為老陽者凡十有二。掛扐之數十有三，除初掛之一為十有二。以四約而三分之，為一者三。一奇象圓而圍三。故三一之中各復有三，而積三三之數則為九。過揲之數三十有六，以四約之，亦得九焉。

〔蔡元定〕掛扐除一，四分四十有八而得其一也。一其十二而三其四也，九之母也。過揲之數，四分四十八而得其三也。三其十二而九其四也，九之子也，皆徑一而圍三也。

children of 9, all with diameter of 1 and circumference of 3.

This is the Greater *Yang* of the Four Images, residing in the number 1 and containing the number 9.

Figure 16

Above (Fig. 16) are all twenty-eight cases of two odds and one even, with the even as ruler, making the younger *yin*. The number of stalks placed between the fingers is 17; subtracting the single 1 makes 16. Dividing 4 by 3 yields two 1s and one 2. A 1 represents a circle, and we use all of it. Thus of the two 1s each contains 3. Two pairs represent a square, and we use half of them. Thus the single 2 contains 2 in it, and the sum of two 3s and one 2 is 8. The number that has been counted off is 32 [49 - 17]; grouping this by fours also yields 8.

> [Ts'ai Yüan-ting:] Subtracting 1 from those placed between the fingers [17], or multiplying 4 by 4, or multiplying 12 by 1 and adding 4, yield the mother of 8. The number of stalks counted off [32], or 8 times 4, or multiplying 12 by 3 and subtracting 4, yields the children of 8.

This is the younger *yin* of the Four Images, residing in 2 and containing 8.

Figure 17

Above (Fig. 17) are all twenty cases of two evens and one odd, with the odd as ruler, making the younger *yang*. The number placed between the fingers is 21. Subtracting the first 1 makes 20. Dividing 4 by 3 yields two 2s and one 1. Two

既四象太陽居一含九之數也。

圖注十六

　右兩奇一耦，以耦為主，為少陰者凡二十有八。掛扐之數十有七，除初掛之一為十有六。以四約而三分之，為一者二，為二者一。一奇象圓而用其全，故二一之中各復有三。二耦象方而用其半，故一二之中復有二焉，而積二三一二數則為八。過揲之數三十有二。以四約之亦得八焉。

〔蔡元定〕掛扐除一，四其四也。自一其十二者而進四也，八之母也。過揲之數，八其四也，自三其十二者而退四也，八之子也。

即四象少陰居二含八之數也。

圖注十七

　右兩耦一奇，以奇為主，為少陽者凡二十。掛扐之數二十有一。除初掛之一為二十。以四約而三分之，為二者二，為一者一。二耦象方而用其半，故二二之中，各復有二。一奇象圓而用其全。故一三之中，復有三焉

I-hsüeh ch'i-meng

pairs represent a square, and we use half of it. Thus the two 2s each contain 2. A single 1 represents a circle, and we use all of it. Thus the single 1 has 3 in it, and the sum of two 2s and one 3 is 7. The number of stalks already counted off is 28 [49 - 21]; grouping this by fours also yields 7.

> [Ts'ai Yüan-ting:] Subtracting 1 from those placed between the fingers, or multiplying 5 by 4, or from 2 times 12 subtracting 4, yields the mother of 7. The number of stalks counted off [28], or 7 times 4, or adding 4 to 2 times 12, yields the children of 7.

This is the younger *yang* of the Four Images, residing in 3 and containing 7.

Figure 18

Above (Fig. 18) are the four cases of three evens making the mature *yin* [6]. The number placed between the fingers is 25; subtracting the single 1 makes 24. Dividing 4 by 3 yields three 2s. Two pairs represent a square, and we use half of it. Thus the three 2s each have 2, and the sum of three twos is 6. The number already counted off is 24 [249 - 25]; grouping this by fours also yields 6.

> [Ts'ai Yüan-ting:] Subtracting 1 from those placed between the fingers yields the mother of 6. The number already counted off [24] is the children of 6, each having two times what is gotten by dividing 48 by 4, or doubling 12, or multiplying 4 by 6. Each has a circumference [perimeter] of 4, and we use half.

，而積二二一三之數則為七。過揲之數，二十有八，以四約之亦得七焉。

〔蔡元定〕掛扐除一，五其四也，自兩其十二者，而退四也，七之母也。過揲之騷數七其四也，自兩其十二者而進四也，七之子也。

即四象少陽居三含七之數也。

圖注十八

右三耦為老陰者四。掛扐之數二十有五。除初掛之一為二十有四。以四約而三分之，為二者三。二耦象方而用其半。故三二之中各，復有二，而積三二之數則為六。過揲之數亦二十有四。以四約之亦得六焉。

掛扐除一，六之母也。過揲之數，六之子也。四分四十有八而各得二也，兩其十二而六其也。皆圍四而用半也。

I-hsüeh ch'i-meng

This is the Greater *Yin* of the Four Images, residing in 4 and containing 6.[112]

These four [types of lines] are all obtained by means of the three Changes and the method of placing the stalks. Thus the Classic says, "In the second space then place again."[113] It also says, "Four operations complete a Change."[114] This indication is very clear. Although the commentaries are not detailed discussions, nevertheless the discussions of the monk I-hsing, Pi Chung-ho, and Ku T'uan, as recorded by Liu Yü-hsi, have completed them.[115] Various scholars of recent times have discussions concerning the placing of stalks only in the first Change, and not in the next two Changes. If we examine the Classic, we see that placing stalks by holding between the fingers only six times does not correspond with the meaning of the second intercalary month every five years. Moreover, the latter two Changes would only have three operations [if this were correct]. Thus it is mistaken.

Also, using the ancient method, then among the three Changes we take the first Change as odd and the latter two Changes as even; odd because the remainder is 5 or 9, even because the remainder is 4 or 8. Of the remainders 5 and 9, there are three cases of 5 and one of 9. This is the meaning of the circumference of 3 and the diameter of 1. Of the remainders 4 and 8, there are two cases of each. This is the meaning of the perimeter of 4, using half. After the three Changes, in the Mature the *yang* is plentiful and the *yin* is meager. In the Young, *yang* is few and *yin* is many. These are all natural patterns and images.

> Ts'ai Yüan-ting says: Starting with fifty milfoil stalks, remove one and divide into two, place one and count off by fours, making three odds and two evens. These are the natural numbers,

即四象太陰居含六之數也。

　凡此四者，皆以三變，皆掛之法得之。蓋經曰："再而後掛"。又曰："四營而成易"。其指甚明。注疏雖不詳說，然劉禹錫所記僧一行畢中和顧彖之說亦已備矣。近世諸儒，乃有前一變獨掛後二變不掛之說。考之於經，乃為六扐而後掛，不應五歲再閏之義。且後兩變又止三營。蓋已誤矣。

　且用舊法，則三變之中，又以前一變為奇，後二變為耦。奇故其餘五九，耦故其餘四八。餘五九者，五三而九一。亦圍三徑一之義也。餘四八者，四八皆二。亦圍四用半之義也。三變之後，老者陽饒而陰乏，少者陽少而陰多。亦皆有自然之法象焉。

　　蔡元定曰。"案五十之蓍虛一分二，掛一揲四，為奇者三，為耦者二。是天三地二自然之數。而三揲之變，老陽老陰之數本皆八。合之得十六。陰

Heaven's 3 and Earth's 2, of the three Changes that are counted off. The root of the frequency of the mature *yang* and mature *yin* is 8; combined they are 16 [see Table 1, note 115]. *Yin* and *yang* are active when mature; yet the nature of *yin* is fundamentally still. Therefore it takes 4 and returns it to the mature *yang*. This is why the frequency of mature *yin* is 4 and the frequency of mature *yang* is 12 [i.e. they both are originally 8]. The root of the frequencies of young *yang* and young *yin* is 24; combined they are 48. *Yin* and *yang* are still when young; yet the nature of *yang* is fundamentally active. Therefore it takes 4 and returns it to the young *yin*. This is why the frequency of young *yang* is 20 and the frequency of young *yin* is 28 [i.e. they both are originally 24].

Yang functions when mature and does not function when young. Thus of the 64 Changes [i.e. Major Changes, or numerical "types" of lines; see Table 1], those that function are 16 Changes [i.e. the mature lines]. Grouping them into fours [four groups of four each], we see that *yang* functions in three [quarters, or 12] and *yin* functions in one [quarter, or 4]. Now, one odd and one even opposing each other is the substance of *yin* and *yang*. Three *yang* and one *yin*, with one abundant and one deficient, is [or makes possible] the functioning of *yin* and *yang*. Therefore of the Four Seasons, spring, summer and autumn give life to things, while winter does not give life to things. In Heaven and Earth, East, West and South are visible, while North is invisible. From man's point of view also, the front, left and right are visible, while the back is invisible.

陽以老為動，而陰性本靜。故以四歸於老陽。此老陰之數所以四，老陽之數所以十二也。少陽少陰之數本皆二十四。含之四十八。陰陽以少為靜，而陽性本動。故以四歸於少陰。此少陽之數所以二十，而少陰之數所以二十八也。

陽用老而不用少。故六十四變，所用清b者十六變。又以四約之陽用其三，陰用其一。蓋一奇一耦對待者，陰陽之體陽三陰一，一饒一乏者，陰陽之用。故四時春夏秋生物，而冬不生物。天地東西南可見，而北不可見。人之瞻視，亦前與左右可見而背不可見也。

When the number placed between the fingers and the number counted off are both 6 times 4 or 2 times 12 this is the mature *yin*.

When we start from the mature *yang*'s number placed between the fingers [12] and add a 4, this is 4 times 4, or 12 plus 4. When we subtract 4 from its number already counted off [36], this is 8 times 4, or 3 times 12 minus a 4. This is called young *yin*.

When we subtract a 4 from mature *yin*'s number placed between the fingers [24], this is 5 times 4, or 2 times 12 discarding 4. Adding 4 to its number counted off [24], this is 7 times 4, or 2 times 12 plus 4. This is called young *yang*.[118]

The two elders are the poles (*chi*) of *yin* and *yang*. The differences between the corresponding numbers of the two ultimates [mature *yang* and mature *yin* in Table 2] are 12. If we divide this by 3, and, starting with the ultimate of *yang* add this [4] to its number placed between the fingers, and subtract it from its number counted off, then each will move by 1/3 [of 12], and this will result in the young *yin*. If we start with the ultimate of *yin* and subtract this [4] from its number placed between the fingers, and add it to its number counted off, then each will move by 1/3 [of 12], and this will result in young *yang*.

The mature *yang* resides in 1 and contains 9. Therefore its 12 stalks placed between the fingers are the fewest, and the 36 stalks counted off are the most numerous. The young *yin* resides in 2 and contains 8. Therefore its 16 stalks placed between the fingers are the next fewest, and the 32 counted off are the next most numerous. The young *yang* resides in 3 and contains 7. Therefore its 20 placed between the fingers

掛扐過揲之數，皆六其四也，兩其十二者，為老陰。

自老陽之掛扐而增一四，則是四其四也。一其十二而又進一四也。自其過揲者而損一四，則是八其四也，三其十二而損一四也。此所謂少陰者也。

自老陰之掛扐而損一四，則是五其四也，兩其十二而去一四也。自其過揲而增一四，則是七其四也，兩其十二而進一四也。此所謂少陽者也。

二老者，陰陽之極也。二極之閒。相距之數凡十有二。而三分之，自陽之極而進其掛扐，退其過揲，各至於三之一，則為少陰。自陰之極，而退其掛扐，進其過揲，各至於三之一，則為少陽。

老陽居一而含九，故其掛扐十二為最少，而過揲三十六為最多。少陰居二而含八，故其掛扐十六為次少，而過揲三十二為次多。少陽居三而含七，故其掛扐二十為稍多，而

are slightly more, and the 28 counted off are slightly fewer. The mature *yin* resides in 4 and contains 6. Therefore its 24 placed between the fingers are the most numerous and its 24 counted off are the fewest.

Now, *yang* is odd and *yin* is even. This is why the number placed between the fingers in mature *yang* are the fewest [12] and in mature *yin* are the most numerous [24]. The two younger ones [16 and 20], one greater and one lesser, lie together in the center. Here we consider the few to be valuable [i.e. because it is *yang*].

Yang is full and *yin* is empty. This is why the number counted off in mature *yang* is most numerous, and in mature *yin* is fewest. The two younger ones [32 and 28], one greater and one lesser, lie together in the center. Here we consider the many to be valuable.

In all of this it is not a case of *yin* and *yang* as two things alternating between decline and growth. Within the one thing these two parts are each things, alternating between decline and growth.[119] Their relations of low and high are like a weight and balance; their relations of division and combination are like tally slips. Certainly this is something that is not within the ability of individual human wisdom to make happen by choice. Rather, the numbers of stalks placed between the fingers are the causes of the 7, 8, 9 and 6, and the numbers of stalks counted off are the results of the 7, 8, 9 and 6. The effects vary between being light and heavy. Some want to do away with placing stalks between the fingers, and only use the numbers of stalks counted off in their determinations. However, this is to set aside the root and take the branch; to discard the essential and get into

過揲二十八為稍少。老陰居四而含六，故其掛扐二十四為極多，而過揲亦二十四為極少。

蓋陽奇而陰耦。是以掛扐之數老陽極少，老陰極多，而二少者，一進一退而交於中焉。此其以少為貴者也。

陽實而陰虛，是以過揲之數，老陽極多，老陰極少，而二少者亦一進一退而交於中焉。此其以多為貴者也。

凡次不唯陰之與陽。既為二物，而迭為消長。而其一物之中，此二端者又各自為一物，而迭為消長。其相與低昂如權衡其相與判合如符契。固有非人之私智所能取舍而有無者。而況掛扐之數，乃七八九六之原，而過揲之數，乃七八九六之委。其勢又有輕重之不同。而或者乃欲廢置掛扐而獨以過揲之數為斷。則是舍本而取末，去約以就繁而不

I-hsüeh ch'i-meng

complications, not knowing that it cannot be done. How can this not be mistaken?

Master Shao said:

> 5 and 4 occur 4 times. Discarding the number of the one placed between the fingers, we then have 4 times 3 or 12. 9 and 8 occur 8 times. Discarding the number of the one placed between the fingers, we then have 4 times 6 or 24. 5 and 8 occur 8 times, and 9 and 4 occur 8 times. Discarding the number of the one placed between the fingers we then have 4 times 5, or 20. 9 and 4 occur 4 times, and 5 and 4 occur 8 times. Discarding the number of the one placed between the fingers, we then have 4 times 4, or 16. Therefore we discard the numbers 3, 4, 5 and 6, in order to derive the stalks 9, 8, 7 and 6.[120]

With these remarks, one line has been completed. For the second, combine the 49 stalks and again divide, place, count off and return to complete one more change. Every three changes completes one line, as in the previous procedure.

The stalks required for Ch'ien are 216. The stalks required for K'un are 144, making a total of 360. This corresponds to the days in the year.[121]

The 216 stalks required for Ch'ien are obtained by adding the stalks of the 6 lines, each of which is 36 [mature *yang*]. The 144 stalks required for K'un are obtained by adding the stalks of the 6 lines, each of which is 24 [mature *yin*]. The "total of 360" is obtained by adding 216 and 144. "This corresponds to the days in the year" means taking each month of 30 days and adding the 12 months to make 360.

知其不可也。豈不誤哉。

邵子曰：

> 五與四四。去掛一之數，則四三十二也。九與八八。去掛一之數，則四六二十四也。五與八八，九與四八。去掛一之數，則四五二十也。九與四四，五與四八去掛一之數，則四四十六也。故去其三四五六之數，以成九八七六之策。

此之謂也，一爻已成。再合四十九策，復分掛揲歸以成一變。每三變而成一爻，並如前法。

乾之策二百一十有六。坤之策百四十有四。凡三百有六十。當期之日。

乾之策二百一十有六者，積六爻之策三十六而得之也。坤之策百四十有四者，積六爻之策，各二十有四而得之也。凡三百六十者，合二百一十有六，百四十有四而得之也。"當期之日"者，每月三十日，合十二月為三百六十也。

蓋以氣言之，則有三百六十六日。以朔言之，則有三百五十四日。今舉氣盈朔虛之中數而言，故曰三百有六十也。然少陽之策二十八，積乾六爻之策，則一百六十八。少陰

I-hsüeh ch'i-meng

In terms of *ch'i* [the solar year] there are 366 days. In terms of lunar months there are 354 days. Focusing on the difference between the *ch'i*'s surplus and the lunar months' deficit, we therefore say 360. However, the stalks of young *yang* are 28; adding the 6 lines of Ch'ien there are 168. The stalks of young *yin* are 32; adding the 6 lines of K'un there are 192. In this passage mentioning only the stalks of mature *yin* and *yang*, the *I* uses 9 and 6 and does not use 7 and 8. However, adding the two younger ones also yields 360.

The stalks in the two parts of the book are 11,520. This corresponds to the number of the myriad things.[122]

"The two parts" are the 64 hexagrams in the two sections of the Classic. There are 192 *yang* lines, each with 36 stalks [counted off], totalling 6,912. There are 192 *yin* lines, each with 24 stalks [counted off], totalling 4,608. Adding the two makes 11,520. If we take young *yang*, then each line has 28 stalks, totalling 5,376. Each line of young *yin* has 32 stalks, totalling 6,144. Adding these also makes 11,520.

Therefore four operations complete a change (*i*); eighteen changes (*pien*) complete a hexagram. The Eight Trigrams are the Minor Completion. Amplifying these, extending each according to its kind, all possible phenomena in the world are covered.[123]

"The four operations" are the four steps of the procedure. Dividing in two is the first operation. Placing one is the second operation. Counting off by fours is the third operation. Returning the remainder is the fourth operation.

之策三十二，積坤六爻之策，則一百九十二。此獨以老陰陽之策為言者，以易用九六，不用七八也。然二少之合，亦三百有六十。

二篇之策，萬有一千萬百二十。當萬物之數也。

"二篇"者，上下經六十四也。其陽爻百九十二，每爻各三十六策，積之得六千九百一十二。陰爻百九十二，每爻二十四策，積之得四千六百八。又合二者，為萬有一千五百二十也。若為少陽則每爻二十八策，凡五千三百七十六。少陰則每爻三十二策，凡六千一百四十四。合之亦為萬一千五百二十也。

是故四營而成易，十有八變而成卦。八卦而小成。引而伸之，觸類而長之，天下之能事畢矣。

"四營"者四次經營也。分二者第一營也。掛一者第二營也。揲四者第三營也。歸奇者第四營也。

"易"變易也，謂揲之一變也。四營成變，三變城爻。一變而得兩儀之象。再變而得四象之象。三變而得八掛之象。一爻而得兩儀之畫。二爻而得四象之畫。三爻而得八卦

I-hsüeh ch'i-meng

"Chang e (*i*)" means alternating change (*pien-i*), referring to each change (*pien*) counted off.[124] Four operations complete a change (*pien*); three changes complete a line. With one change we have a symbol of the Two Modes. With the second change we have a symbol of the Four Images. With the third change we have a symbol of the Eight Trigrams. With one line we have a picture of the Two Modes. With two lines we have a picture of the Four Images. With three lines we have a picture of the Eight Trigrams. With four lines completed we have one of the 16. With five lines completed we have one of the 32. When we come to a total of 72 operations and have completed 18 changes, we then have six lines and can see one of the 64 hexagrams.

However, at the point of 36 operations, or 9 changes, we already have three lines, and the names of the Eight Trigrams can be seen. Thus the inner [lower] trigrams (*chen*) are established. This is what is meant by "Eight Trigrams are the Minor Completion." From this we proceed by extension to another 36 operations and 9 changes, completing three lines and getting a second Minor Completion trigram. Thus the outer [upper] trigrams (*hui*) are completed. With six lines completed, the inner and outer trigrams are done, and the divisions of the 64 hexagrams can be seen. Only then do we observe whether the lines are changing or unchanging, and extend them accordingly. Consequently, the "good fortune and bad fortune, repentance and regret" of all the world's phenomena do not go beyond this.[125]

It reveals the Way and spiritualizes moral action. Therefore we can repay pledges and enshrine spirits.[126]

The Way accords with words and reveals [the proper course of] action by calculating the spiritual. "Repay pledges"

之畫。四爻成而得其十六者之一。五爻成而得其三十二者之一。至於積七十二營而成十有八變，則六爻，見而得乎六十四卦之一矣。

然方其三十六營而九變也，已得三畫，而八卦之名可見。則內卦之為貞者立矣。此所謂"八卦而小成"者也。自是而往，又而伸之，又三十六營九變，以成三畫，而再得小成之卦者一。則外卦之為悔者亦備矣。六爻成，內外卦備。六十四卦之別可見。然後視其爻之變與不變而觸類以長焉。則天下之事，其吉凶悔吝，皆不越乎此矣。

顯道神德行。是故可與酬酢可與祐神矣。

道因辭顯行以數神。"酬酢"者言幽明之相應，如賓主之相交也。"祐神"者言有以祐助神化之功也。

I-hsüeh ch'i-meng

refers to the mutual response of dark and light, like the mutual interaction of guest and host. "Enshrine spirits" refers to assisting the achievement of spiritual transformation.

Concerning Mr. Ts'ai's explanation in this chapter of the "three odds and two evens [above, p. 39]." In the first counting-off, the left hand's remaining 1, remaining 2, and remaining 3 are all odd, while the remaining 4 is even. In the second and third counting-off, the remaining 3 is also even. Therefore he says, "three odds and two evens."

卷內蔡氏說為奇者三，為耦者二。蓋凡初揲，左手餘一餘二餘三皆為奇。餘四為耦。至再揲三揲，則餘三者亦為耦。故曰奇三而耦二也。

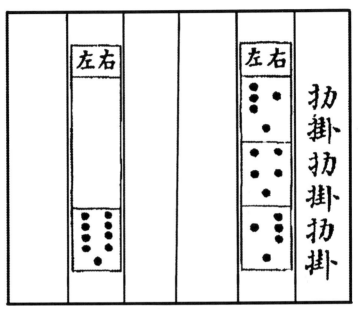

Figure 13

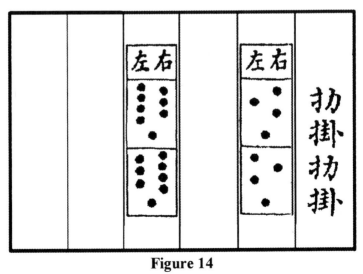

Figure 14

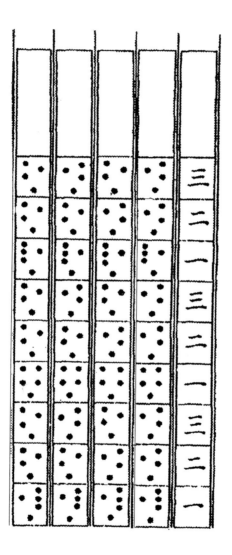

Figure 15

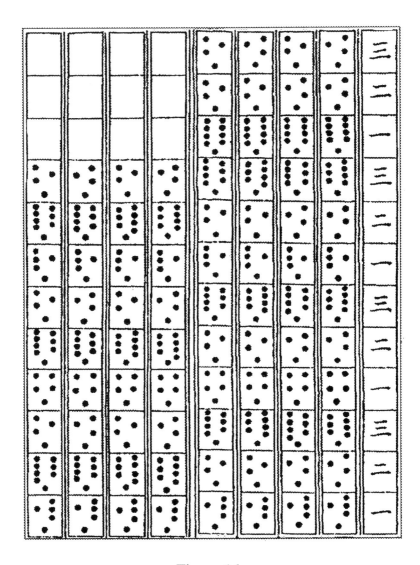

Figure 16

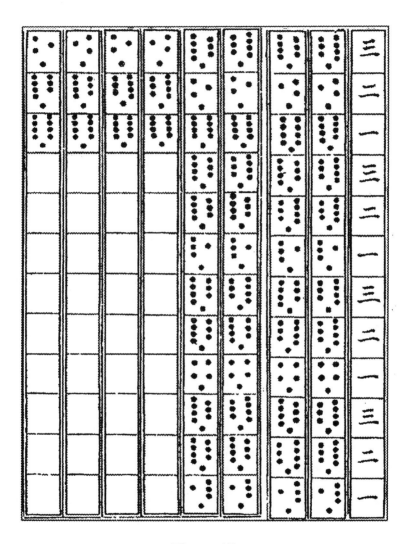

Figure 17

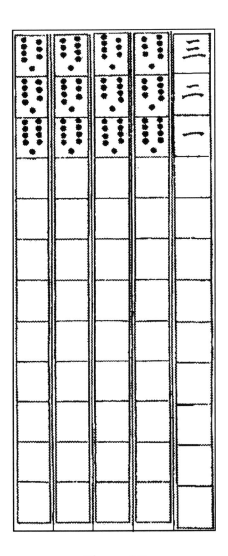

Figure 18

I-hsüeh ch'i-meng

IV. Examining the Prognostications of the Changes[127]

> The Ch'ien hexagram: Using 9s shows a flight of dragons without heads. Good fortune. The Image says: Using 9s, Heavenly virtue cannot be the head.
>
> The K'un hexagram: Using 6s, it is beneficial to be eternally steady. The Image says: Using 6s, be eternally steady for a great conclusion."[128]

"Using 9s" and "using 6s" means a changing hexagram throughout. It refers to the *yang* lines all using 9 and not using 7, and the *yin* lines all using 6 and not using 8. Using 9, the mature *yang* therefore changes into young *yin*. Using 6, the mature *yin* therefore changes into young *yang*. They do not use 7 and 8, and so the young *yang* and young *yin* do not change.

That this only speaks of the two hexagrams Ch'ien and K'un is due to their being at the head of all the hexagrams. They also are the hexagrams of pure *yang* and pure *yin*. Thus the Sage [Confucius] appended them with [additional] texts.[129] When we get Ch'ien with all six lines as 9 [in divination], or K'un with all six lines as 6, we then use this as the prognostication. Thus "a flight of dragons without heads" is the image of *yang* completely changing to *yin*. "It is beneficial to be eternally steady" is the meaning of *yin* completely changing to *yang*. [These statements] abundantly illustrate the category of six lines changing.

> [Ts'ai Yüan-ting:] Master Ou-yang [Hsiu][130] said: "What is the meaning of Ch'ien and K'un using 9 and 6?"

考變占第四

乾卦用九見群龍元無首。吉象曰："用九天德不可為首也"。

坤卦用六利永貞。象曰："用六永貞以大終也。"

"用九""用六"者，變卦之凡例也。言凡陽爻皆用九而不用七。陰爻皆用六而不用八。用九，故老陽變為少陰。用六，故老陰變為少陽。不用七八，

故少陽少陰不變。獨於乾坤二卦言之者，以其在諸卦之首。又為純陽純陰之卦也。聖人因繫以辭。使遇乾而六爻皆九，遇坤而六爻皆六者，即此而占之。蓋群龍無首，則陽皆變陰之象。"利永貞"，則陰皆變陽之義也。餘見六爻變例。

〔蔡元定〕歐陽子曰："乾坤之用九用六何謂也。"

"Reply: The lines of Ch'ien are 7 and 9; the lines of K'un are 8 and 6. 9 and 6 change, while 7 and 8 do nothing. The Way of Change predicts these changes. Therefore we name the lines by their prognostications; it does not mean that all six lines are 9 or 6.[131] As for their casting, 7 and 8 are always more frequent, and 9 and 6 are always less frequent. The occurrence and non-occurrence of 9 and 6 cannot be uninstructive. This is so for all 64 hexagrams. It is especially apparent in Ch'ien and K'un, and so the rest can be understood."

In my humble opinion, this explanation manifests the shortcomings of previous scholars. What is most valuable about this is the theory that 7 and 8 are more frequent and 9 and 6 are less frequent. We also see the divination method of that time: [only] three changes make a hexagram, as in the theory of [the Buddhist scholar] I-hsing.

Any hexagram may have all unchanging lines. In that case we prognosticate on the basis of the original hexagram's *T'uan* statement, taking the inner hexagram as *chen* [the question, or present situation] and the outer hexagram as *hui* [the prognostication].

[Ts'ai Yüan-ting:] The *T'uan* statement is the statement under the hexagram.[132] [For example,] K'ung Ch'eng-tzu divined to establish the Duke of Wei's son, Yüan [as successor], and obtained Chun [hexagram 3], which says: "It is beneficial to establish princes."[133] And Po of Ch'in attacked Chin, and divined for it, obtaining Ku [hexagram 18], which has wind as the lower trigram (*chen*) and mountain as the upper trigram (*hui*).[134]

曰：乾爻七九，坤爻八六。九六變而七八無為。易道占其變。故以其所占者名爻。不謂六爻皆九六也。

及其筮也，七八常多。而九六常少。有無九六者焉，此不可以不釋也。六十四卦皆然。特於乾坤見之，則餘可知耳。

愚案此說發明先儒所未到。最為有功，其論七八多而九六少。又見當時占法。三變皆，如一行說，

凡卦六爻皆不變。則占本卦彖辭，而以內卦為貞，外卦為悔。

〔蔡元定〕彖辭為卦下之辭。孔成子筮立衛公子元，遇屯曰："利建侯。"秦伯伐晉，筮之遇蠱，曰貞風也，其悔山也。

I-hsüeh ch'i-meng

When only one line changes, we take the statement of the original hexagram's changing line as the prognostication.

> [Ts'ai Yüan-ting:] Ch'eng Shao-sui said [e.g.] "Pi Wan obtained Chun [hexagram 3] going [changing] to Pi [hexagram 8], with the first 9 changing.[135] Ts'ai Mo obtained Ch'ien [hexagram 1] going to T'ung-jen [hexagram 13], with the 9 in the second place changing.[136] Duke Wen of Chin obtained Ta-yu [hexagram 14] going to K'uei [hexagram 38], with the 9 in the third place changing.[137] Ch'en Ching-chung obtained Kuan [hexagram 20] going to Pi [hexagram 12], with the 6 in the fourth place changing.[138] Nan K'uai obtained K'un [hexagram 2] going to Pi [hexagram 8], with the 6 in the fifth place changing.[139] Duke Hsien of Chin obtained Kuei-mei [hexagram 54] going to K'uei [hexagram 38], with the upper six changing.[140]

When two lines change, we take the statements of the two changing lines of the original hexagram as the prognostication, but we take the upper line [of the two] as ruler.[141]

> [Tsai Yüan-ting:] In the Classic and the Appendices there is no [such] passage. Extrapolating from what is present [in the text] yields this.

When three lines change, the prognostication is the *T'uan* statement of the original hexagram and the resulting hexagram, and we use the original hexagram as *chen* and the resulting hexagram as *hui*. In the first ten hexagrams [of this sort] we make *chen* the ruler; in the latter ten hexagrams we make *hui* the ruler.

一爻變則以本卦變爻辭占。

〔蔡元定〕沙隨程氏曰："畢萬遇屯之比，初九變也蔡墨遇乾之同人，九二變也。晉文公遇大有之睽，九三變也。陳敬仲遇觀之否，六四變也。南蒯遇坤之比，六五變也。晉公遇歸妹之睽，上六變也。

二爻變則以本卦二變爻辭占，仍以上爻為主。

〔蔡元定〕(經傳無文。今以例推之當如此。)

三爻變則占本卦及之卦之彖辭，。而以本卦為貞之卦為悔。前十卦主貞，後十卦主悔。

I-hsüeh ch'i-meng

> [Ts'ai Yüan-ting:] All those with three lines changing total 20 hexagrams. See the following chart. Ch'eng Sha-sui said:
>
> "The son of the Duke of Chin is important. He divined to acquire a state. He obtained Chun [hexagram 3] as *chen* and Yu [hexagram 16] as *hui*, with all [the rest as] 8s."[142]
>
> Here the first, fourth and fifth, for a total of three lines, changed. The first and fifth used 9 to change, and the fourth used 6 to change. Those that did not change were the second, third and top. In the two hexagrams all others were 8. Thus he says, "all 8s." And Ssu-k'ung Chi-tzu prognosticated, saying, "It is always beneficial to establish princes."[143]

When four lines change, we use the two unchanging lines in the resulting hexagram as the prognostication. But we take the lower line as ruler.

> [Ts'ai Yüan-ting:] The Classic and the Appendices do not contain this line either. Extrapolating from what is present [in the text] yields this.

When five lines change, we use the unchanging line of the resulting hexagram as the prognostication.

> [Ts'ai Yüan-ting:] When Mu Chiang went to the Eastern Palace, she divined and obtained Ken [hexagram 52], with one eight. The diviner (*shih*) said, "This means Ken changing to Sui [hexagram 17]."[144] Thus five lines all changed [all but the second]. Only the second yielded 8, which is why it was unchanging. The proper method is to take "If one clings to the little boy, one loses the great

〔蔡元定〕凡三爻變者。通二十卦。有圖在後。

沙隨程氏曰："晉公子重耳。筮得國。遇貞屯悔豫皆八。"

蓋初與四五凡三爻變也。初與五用九變，四用六變。其不變者二三上。在兩卦皆為八，故云"皆八"。而司空季子占之曰"皆利建侯"。

四爻變則以之卦二不變爻占，仍以下爻為主。

〔蔡元定〕(經傳亦無文。今以例推之當如此。)

五爻變則以之卦不變爻占

(穆姜往東宮，筮遇艮之八。史曰"是謂艮之隨"。蓋五爻皆變。唯二得八，故不變也。法宜以"係小子夫大夫

man" [line 2 of Sui] as the prognostication. But the diviner mistakenly indicated the *T'uan* statement of Sui in his response.[145] So he was wrong.

When six lines change, in the cases of Ch'ien and K'un, the prognostications of both are used. For other hexagrams, the prognostication is the *T'uan* statement of the resulting hexagram.

[Ts'ai Yüan-ting:] Ts'ai Mo said, "Ch'ien changing to K'un says: 'Seeing a flight of dragons without heads is good fortune.'"[146] However, "a flight of dragons without heads" corresponds to K'un's mare, which "at first is lost."[147] K'un's [statement] "It is beneficial to be eternally steady" corresponds to the fact that Ch'ien does not mention what [kind of penetration] is beneficial.[148]

Thus each hexagram can change into sixty-four hexagrams, resulting in 4,096 [combinations of] hexagrams. This is what is meant by "Continuing by extension, adding to each and expanding them, all possible phenomena under Heaven are included."[149] How can we not believe it? We now take the changes [combinations] of the sixty-four hexagrams and arrange them into thirty-two charts (Fig.19). To obtain the first [32] hexagrams we go from beginning to end and from top to bottom. To obtain the last [32] hexagrams we go from the end to the beginning and from bottom to top. The changes in the hexagrams up through the 32nd use the lines of the original hexagram as prognostication. The changes of the hexagrams after the 32nd use the lines of the changed hexagram as prognostication.

，"為占。而史要引隨之彖辭以對則非也。)

六爻變則乾坤占二用。餘卦占之卦彖辭。

〔蔡元定〕"蔡墨曰："乾之坤曰、見群龍無首。吉。是也然群龍無首即坤之牝馬先迷也。坤之利永貞即乾之不言所利也。

於是一卦可變六十四卦，而四千九十六在其中矣。所謂"引而伸之觸類而長之，天下之能事畢矣"。豈不信哉。今以六十四卦之變，列為三十二圖。得初卦者自初而終，自上而下。得末卦者自終而初，自下而上。變在第三十二卦以前者占本卦爻之辭。變在第三十卦以後者，占變卦爻之辭。凡言初終上下者，據圖而言。

[Ts'ai Yüan-ting:] Whenever we speak of earlier and later hexagrams, the order proceeds from the original hexagram.

Figures 19-1 through 19-32

[Below] are the thirty-two charts. By reversing them we have sixty-four charts. Each chart takes one hexagram as ruler and combines it with each of the sixty-four hexagrams, for a total of 4,096 hexagrams. This agrees with the Chiao Kan's *I-lin* (Grove of Changes).[150] But its rational principle is subtle and fine, and consequently there are aspects of it that have not been expressed by former scholars. Those interested should examine it.

〔蔡元定〕言第幾卦前後者從本起。

圖注十九。一至十九。三十二

　　以上三十二圖。反復之則為六十四圖。圖以一卦為主，而各具六十四卦，凡四千幾十六卦。與焦贛易林合。然其條理精密，則有先儒所未發者。臨者詳之。

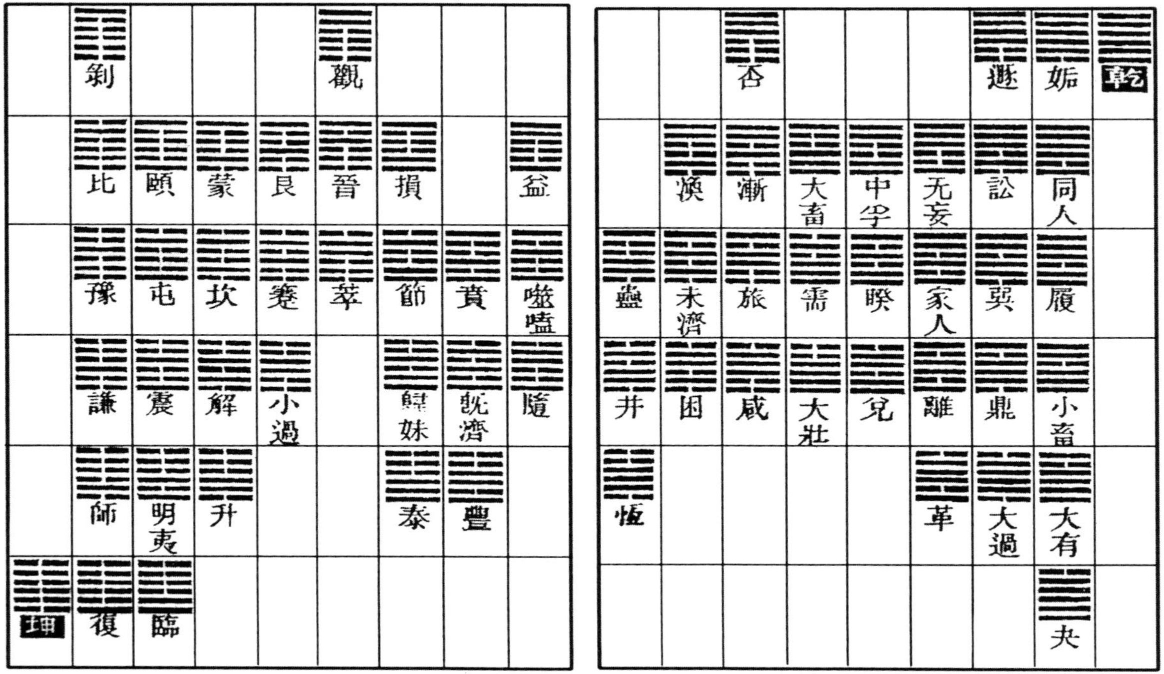
剝 觀
比 頤 蒙 艮 晉 損 益
豫 屯 坎 蹇 萃 節 賁 噬嗑
謙 震 解 小過 歸妹 既濟 隨
師 明夷 升 泰 豐
坤 復 臨
否 遯 姤 乾
渙 漸 大畜 中孚 无妄 訟 同人
蠱 未濟 旅 需 睽 家人 巽 履
井 困 咸 大壯 兌 離 鼎 小畜
恆 革 大過 大有
夬

Figure 4.19.1

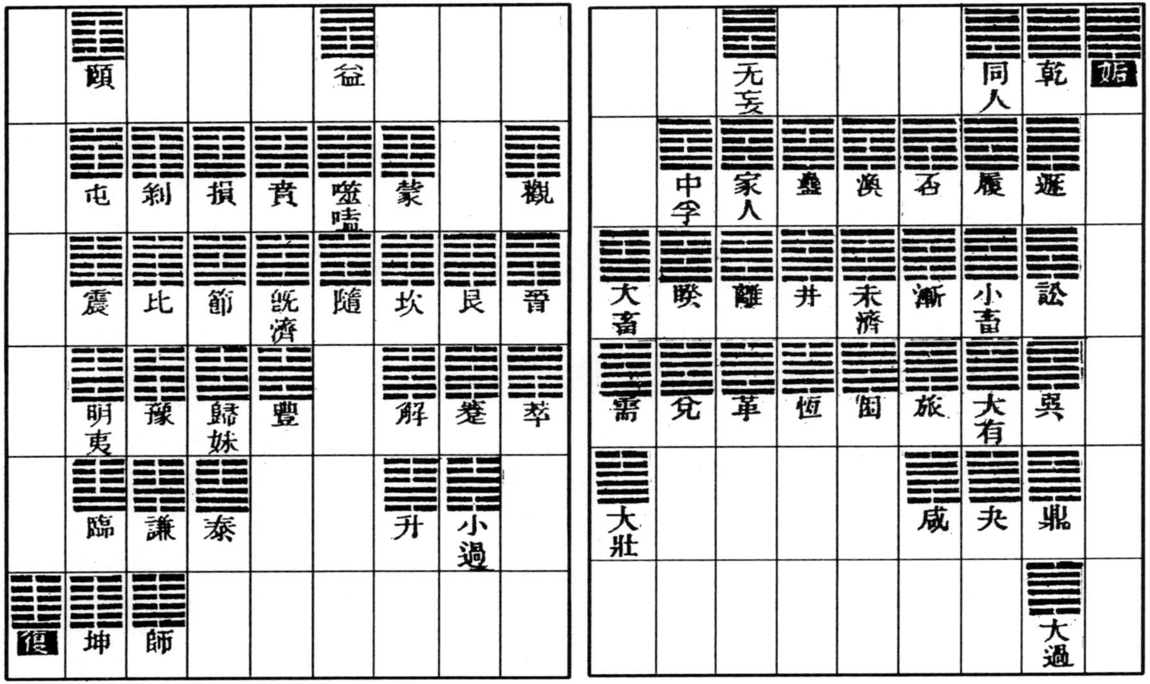
頤
益
屯
剝
損
賁
噬嗑
蒙
觀
震
比
節
既濟
隨
坎
艮
晉
明夷
豫
歸妹
豐
解
蹇
萃
臨
謙
泰
升
小過
復
坤
師
无妄
同人
乾
姤
中孚
家人
蠱
渙
否
履
遯
大畜
睽
離
井
未濟
漸
小畜
訟
需
兌
革
恆
困
旅
大有
巽
大壯
咸
夬
鼎
大過

Figure 4.19.2

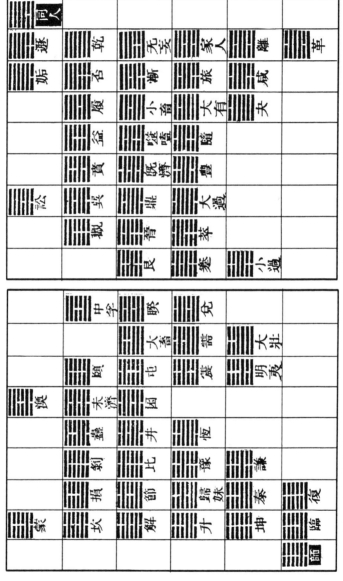

Figure 4.19.3

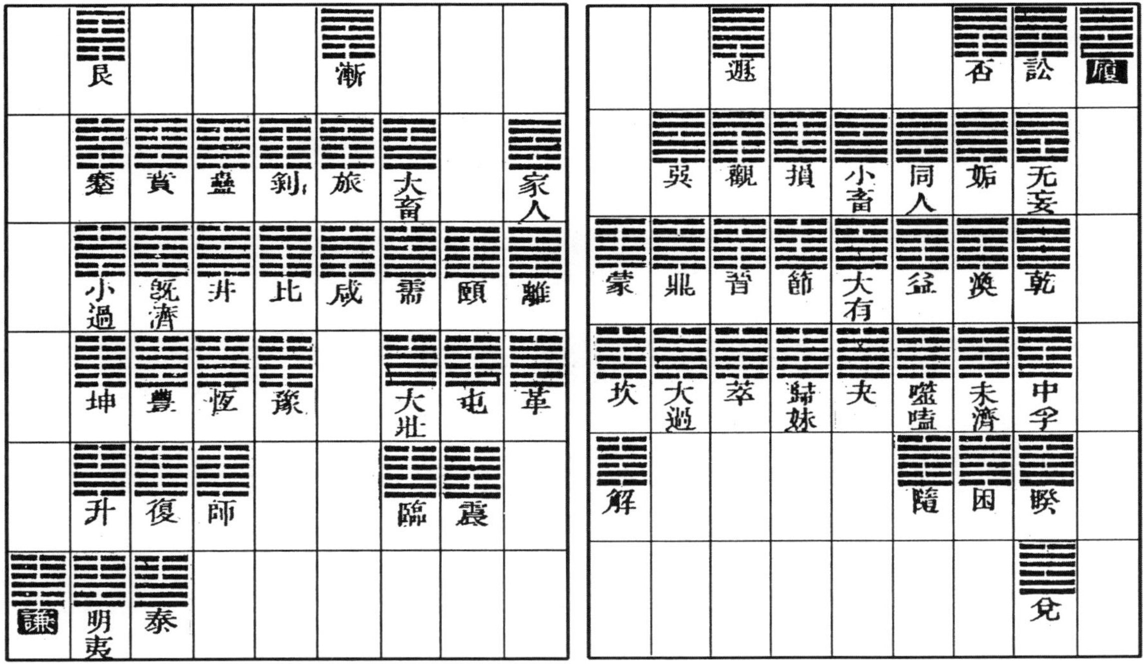
艮 漸
蹇 賁 蠱 剝 旅 大畜 家人
小過 旣濟 井 比 咸 需 頤 離
坤 豐 恆 豫 大壯 屯 革
升 復 師 臨 震
謙 明夷 泰
遯 否 訟 履
巽 觀 損 小畜 同人 姤 无妄
蒙 鼎 晉 節 大有 益 渙 乾
坎 大過 萃 歸妹 夬 噬嗑 未濟 中孚
解 隨 困 睽
兌

Figure 4.19.4

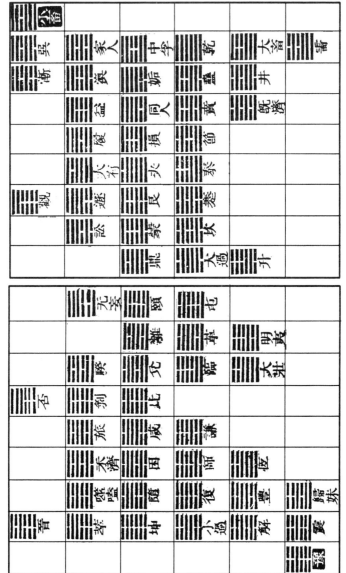

Figure 4.19.5

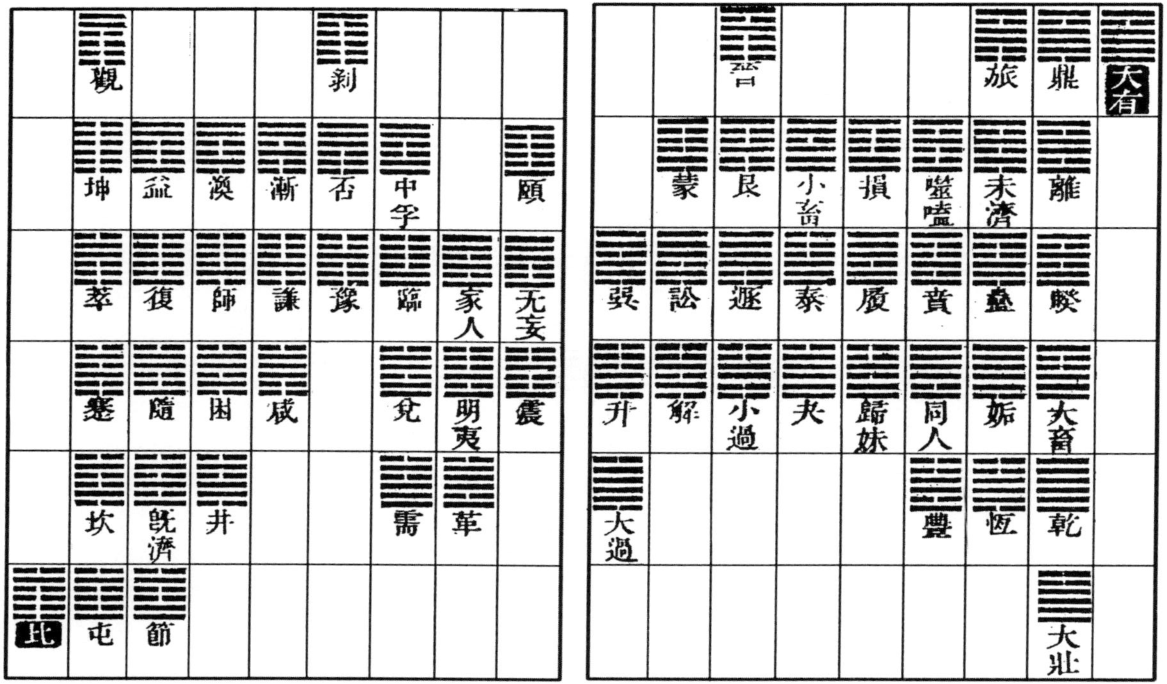
觀 剝
坤 益 渙 漸 否 中孚 頤
萃 復 師 謙 豫 臨 家人 无妄
蹇 隨 困 咸 兌 明夷 震
坎 既濟 井 需 革
比 屯 節
晉 旅 鼎 大有
蒙 艮 小畜 損 噬嗑 未濟 離
巽 訟 遯 泰 履 賁 蠱 睽
升 解 小過 夬 歸妹 同人 姤 大畜
大過 豐 恆 乾
大壯

Figure 4.19.6

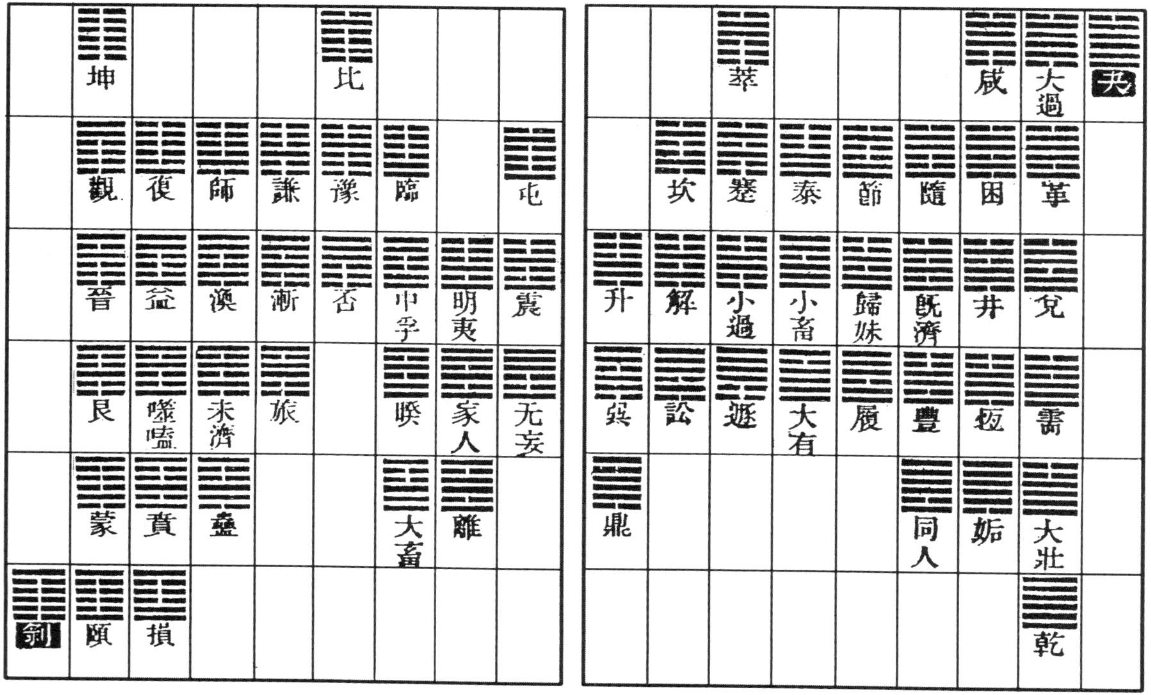

坤
比
觀
復
師
謙
豫
臨
屯
晉
益
渙
漸
否
中孚
明夷
震
艮
噬嗑
未濟
旅
睽
家人
无妄
蒙
賁
蠱
大畜
離
剝
頤
損
萃
咸
大過
夬
坎
蹇
泰
節
隨
困
革
升
解
小過
小畜
歸妹
既濟
井
兌
巽
訟
遯
大有
履
豐
恆
需
鼎
同人
姤
大壯
乾

Figure 4.19.7

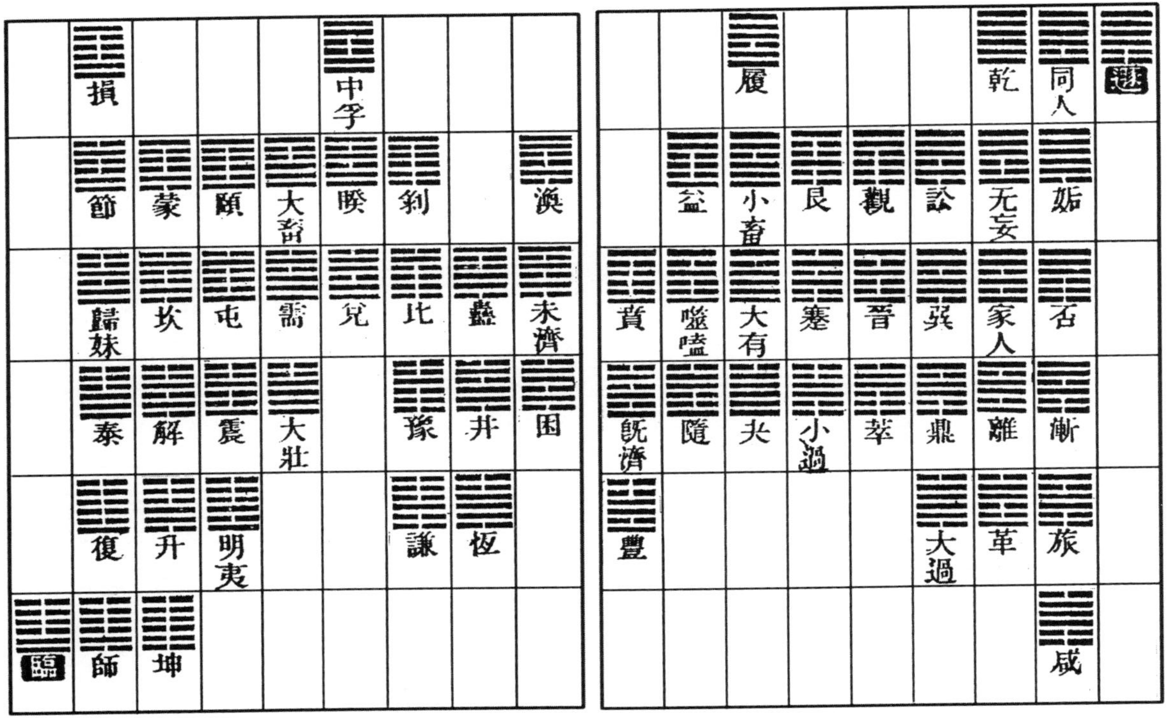
損 中孚
節 蒙 頤 大畜 睽 剝 渙
歸妹 坎 屯 需 兌 比 蠱 未濟
泰 解 震 大壯 豫 井 困
復 升 明夷 謙 恆
臨 師 坤
履 乾 同人 遯
益 小畜 艮 觀 訟 无妄 姤
賁 噬嗑 大有 蹇 晉 巽 家人 否
既濟 隨 夬 小過 萃 鼎 離 漸
豐 大過 革 旅
咸

Figure 4.19.8

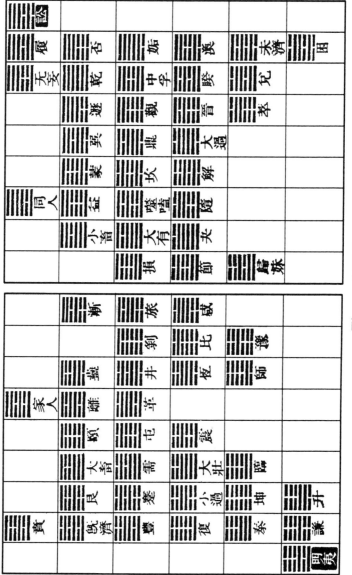

Figure 4.19.9

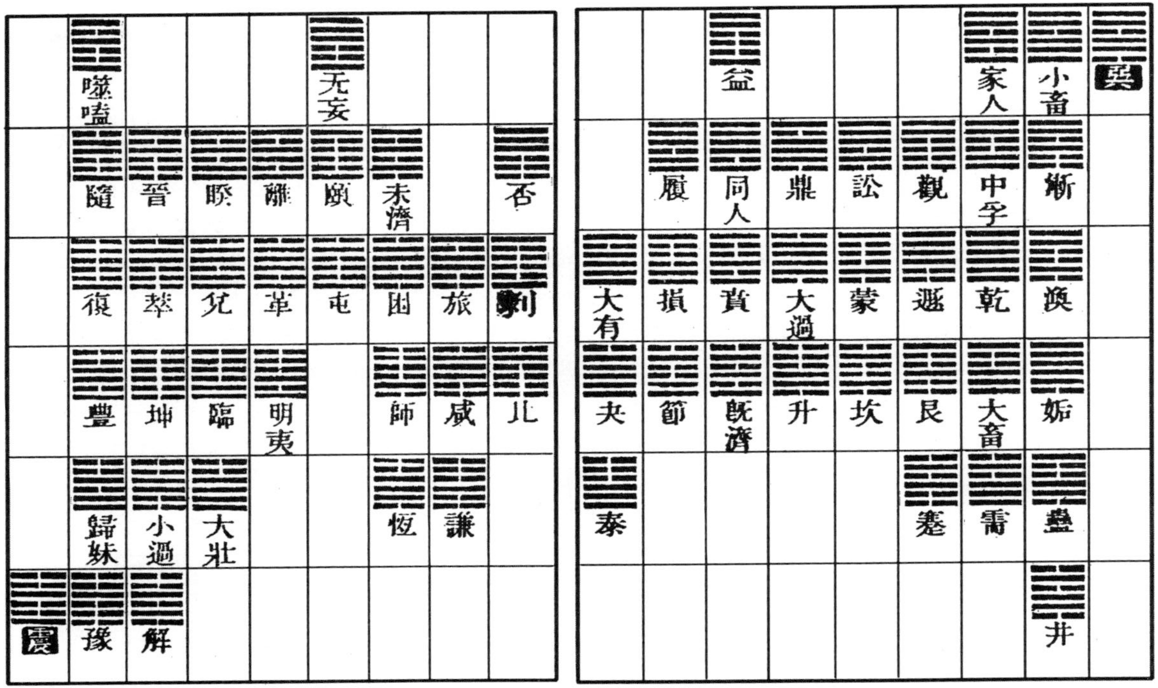

Figure 4.19.10

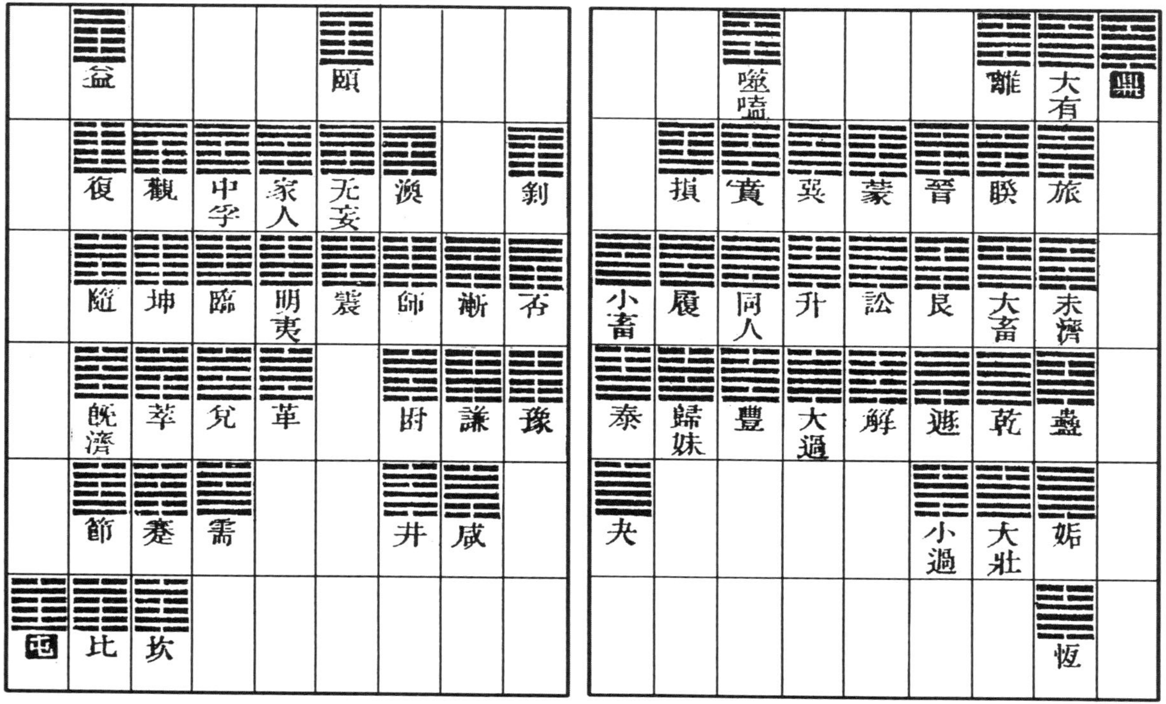

Figure 4.19.11

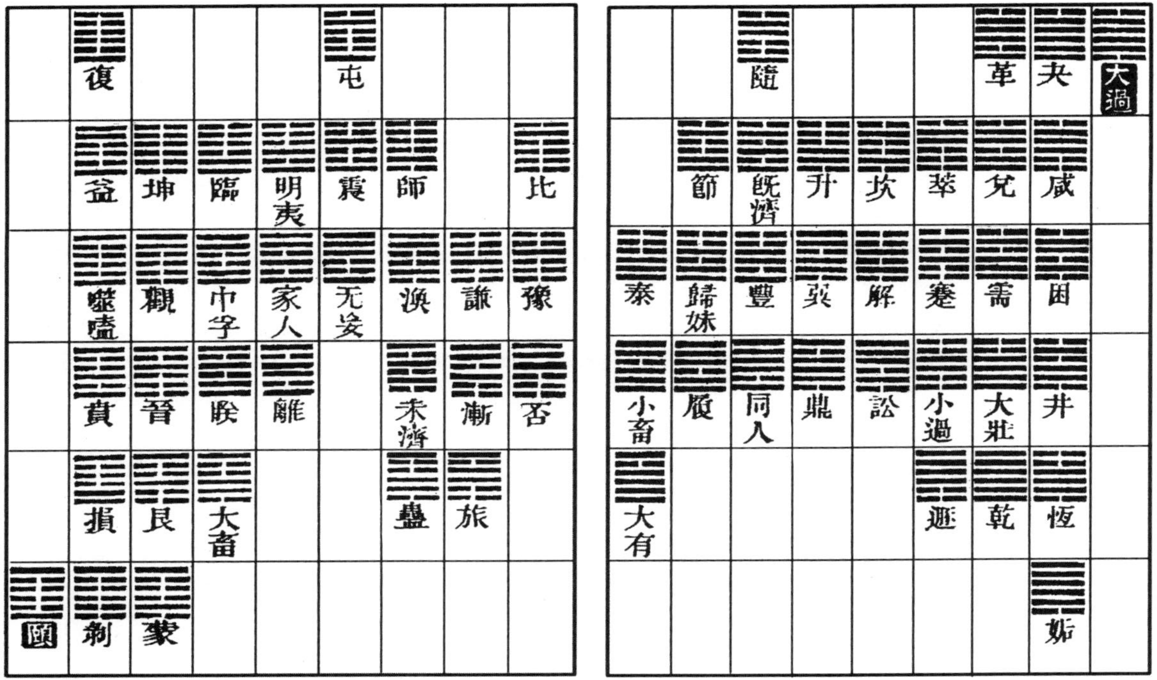

Figure 4.19.12

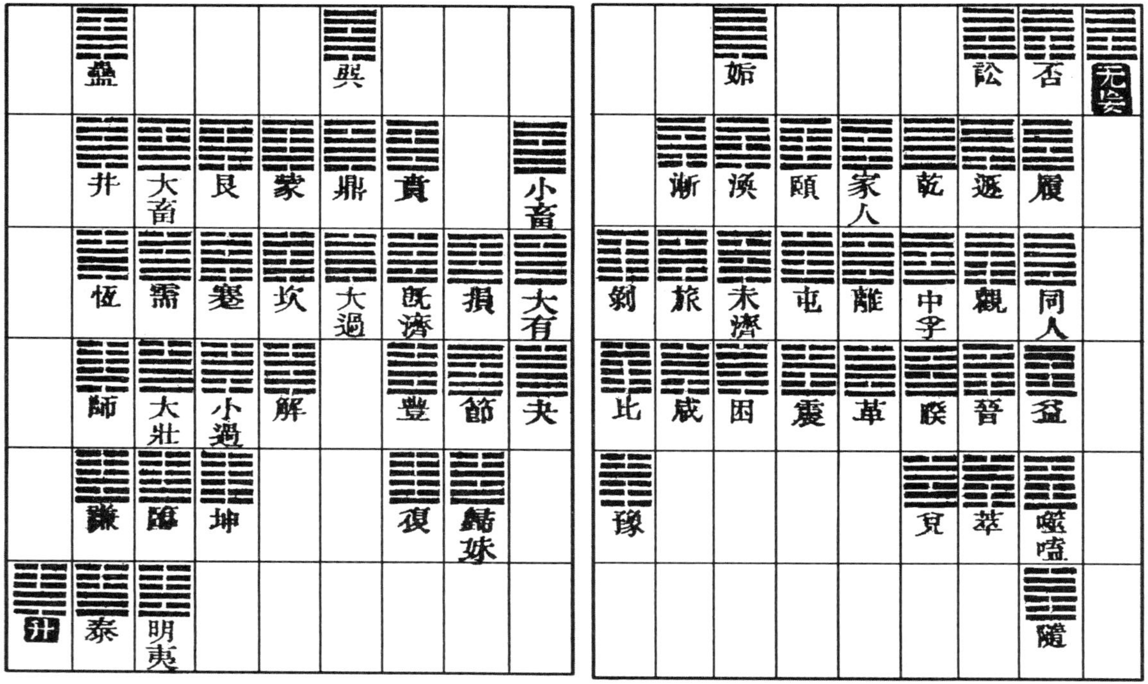

Figure 4.19.13

家人						
漸	小畜	益	同人	賁	既濟	
巽	觀	頤	艮	蒙		
	中孚	乾	大畜	需		
	无妄	頤	屯			
	離	革	明夷			
渙	姤	蠱	井			
	否	剝	比			
		旅	咸	謙		

	履	損	節			
		大有	夬	泰		
	噬嗑	隨	復	豐		
訟	蒙	扶				
	困	大過	升			
	晉	萃	坤	小過		
	睽	兌	恆	大壯	震	
未濟	困	師	巛	豫	歸妹	
					閏	

Figure 4.19.14

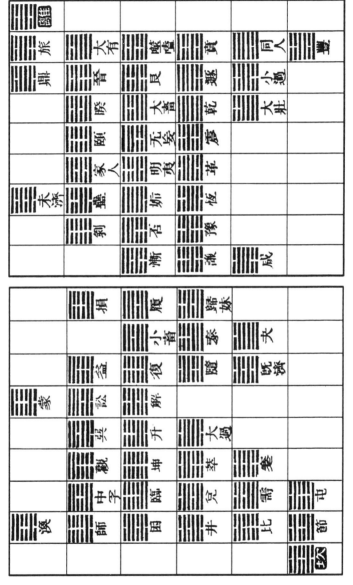

Figure 4.19.15

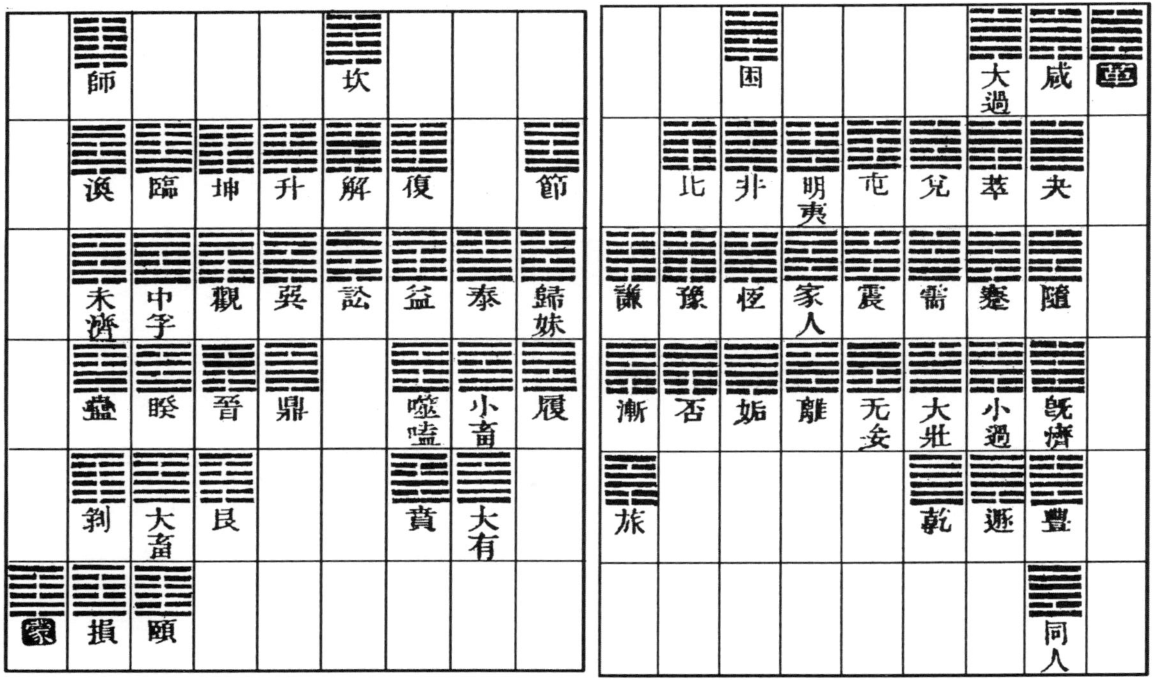

Figure 4.19.16

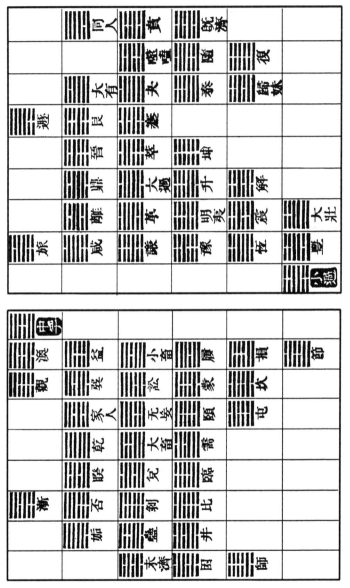

Figure 4.19.17

睽						
未濟	噬嗑	大有	損	頤	歸妹	
晉	鼎	蒙	訟	解		
	離	頤	无妄	震		
	大畜	乾	大壯			
	中孚	履	兌			
旅	剝	否	豚			
	蠱	姤	恆			
		渙	師	困		

	賁	同人	豐			
	益	復	隨			
	小畜	泰	夬	節		
艮	遯	小過				
	觀	坤	萃			
	巽	升	大過	坎		
	家人	明夷	革	屯	需	
漸	謙	咸	比	井	既濟	
					蹇	

Figure 4.19.18

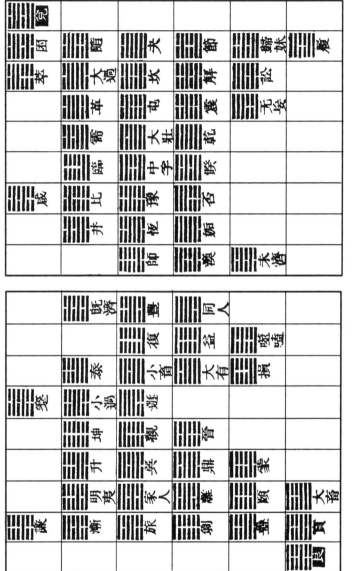

Figure 4.19.19

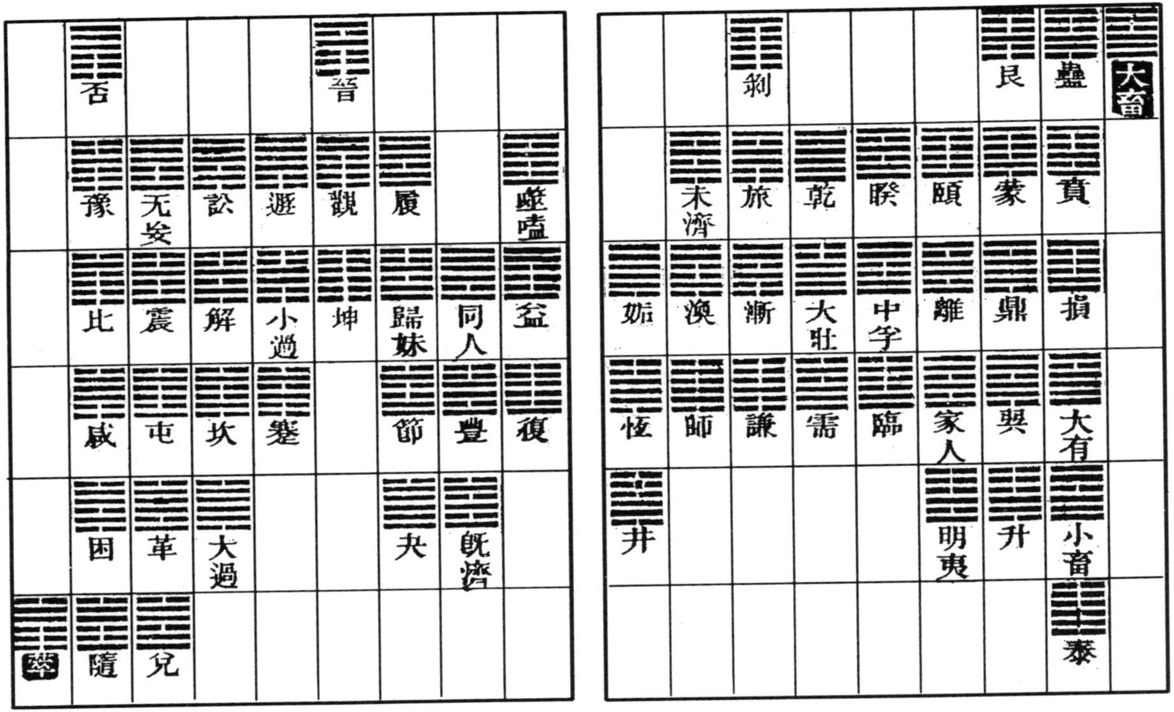

Figure 4.19.20

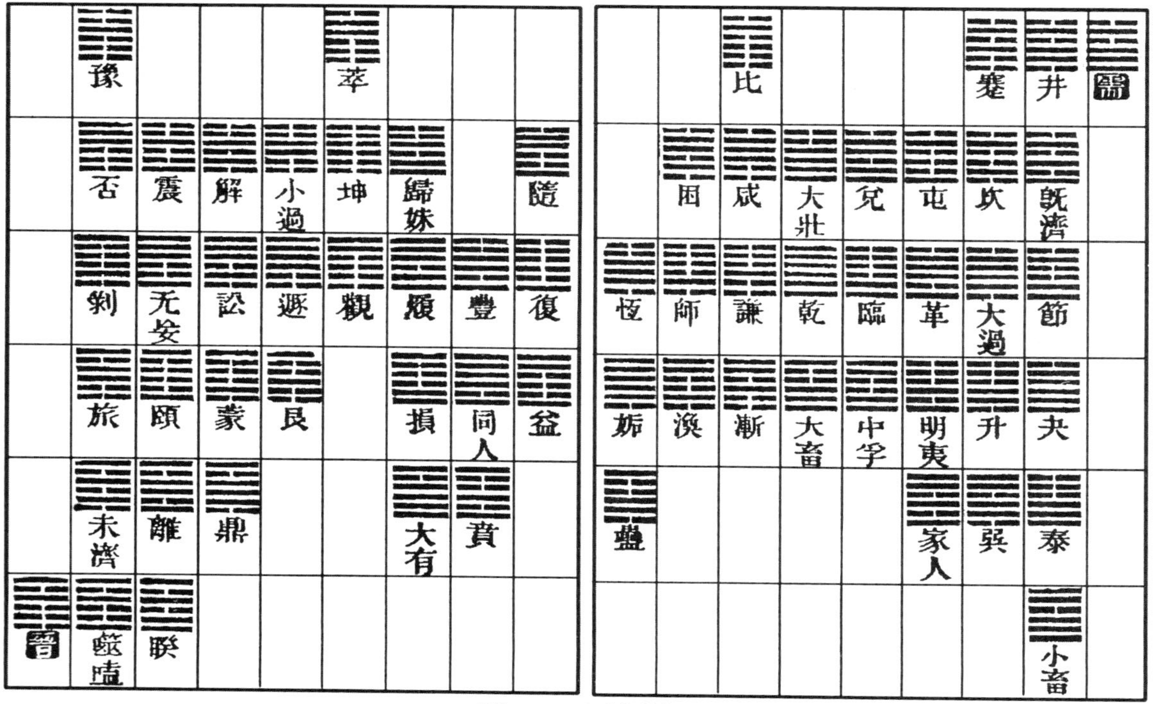

Figure 4.19.21

困						
恆	豐	歸妹	泰	夬	大有	
小過	解	升	大過	鼎		
	震	明夷	革	離		
	臨	兌	睽			
	需	大畜	乾			
豫	謙	咸	旅			
	師	困	未濟			
	井	蠱	姤			

	復	隨	噬嗑			
		既濟	賁	同人		
	節	損	履	小畜		
坤	萃	晉				
	蹇	艮	遯			
	扶	蒙	訟	巽		
	屯	頤	无妄	家人	中孚	
比	剝	否	漸	渙	益	
					觀	

Figure 4.19.22

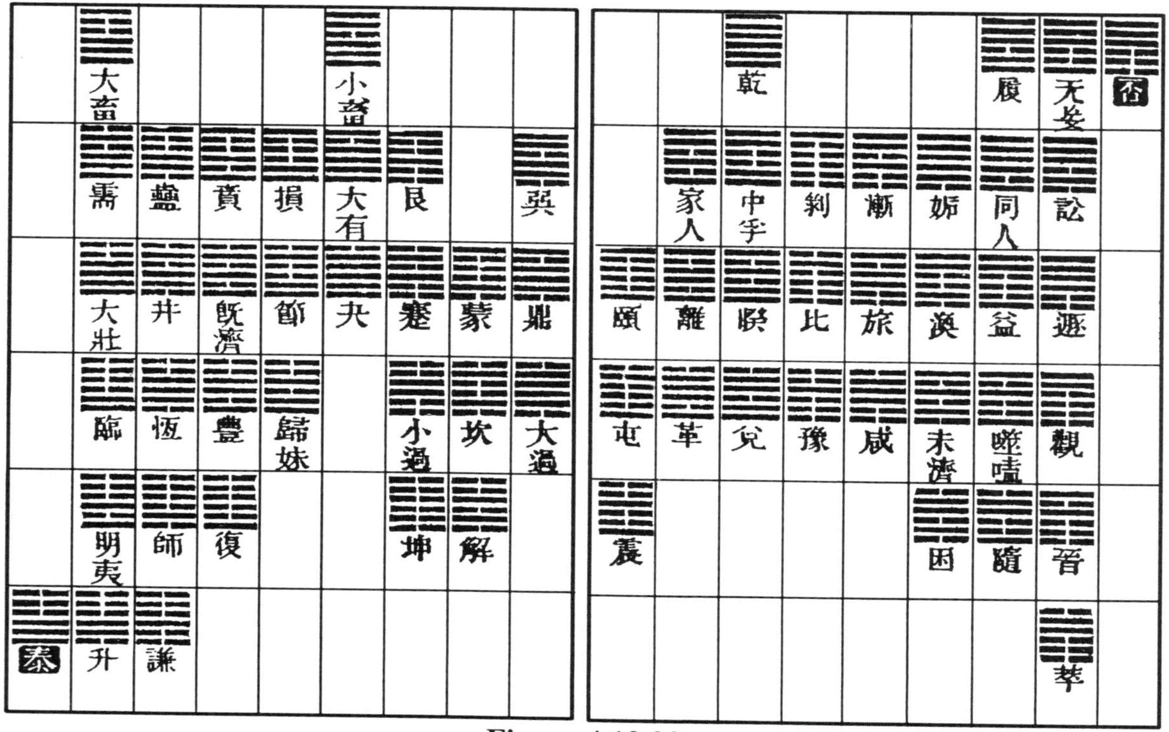

Figure 4.19.23

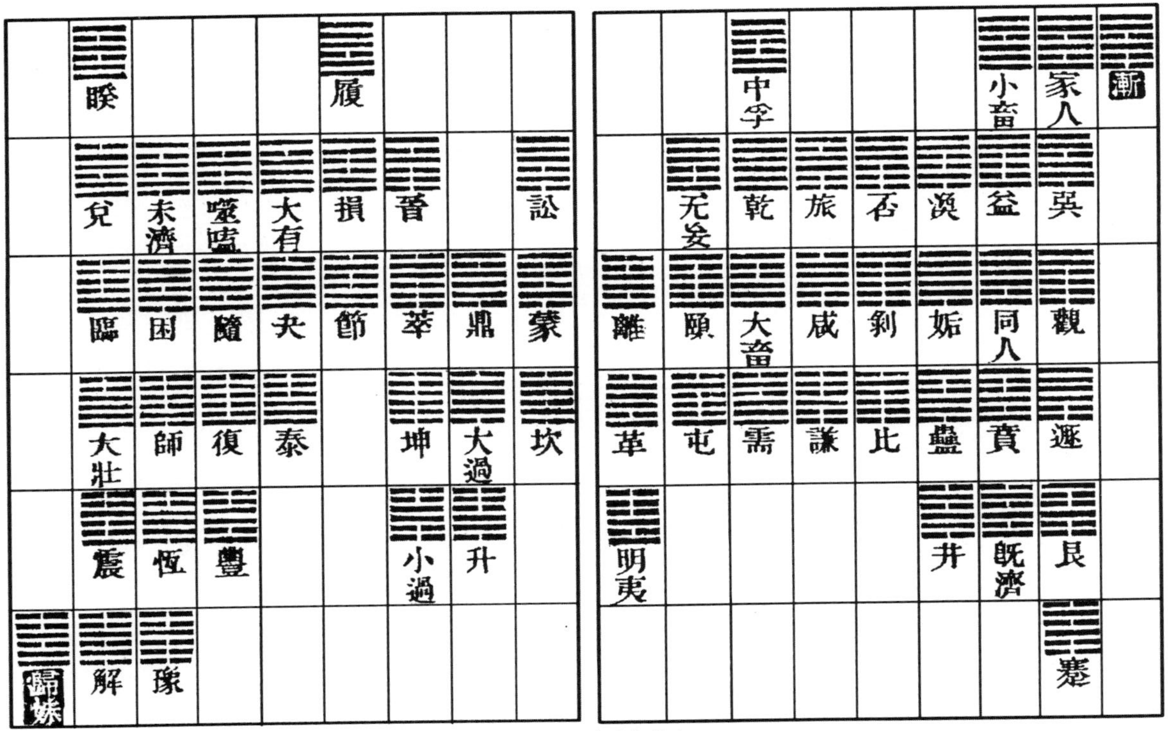

Figure 4.19.24

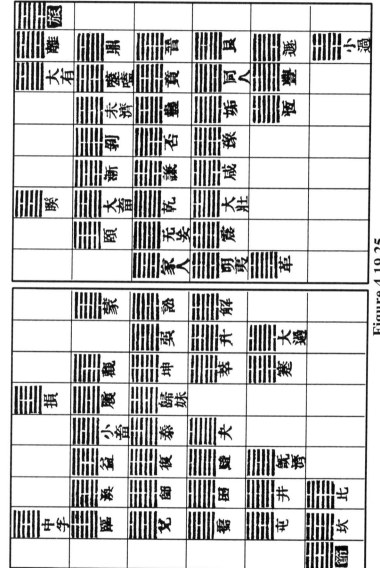

Figure 4.19.25

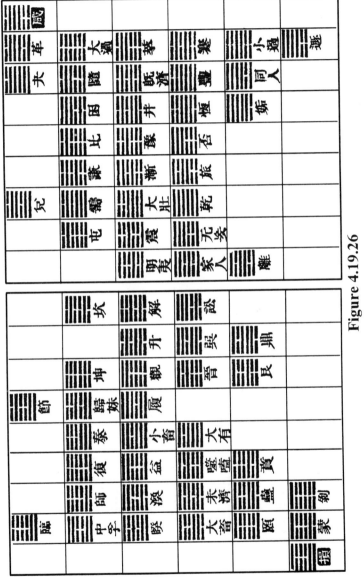

Figure 4.19.26

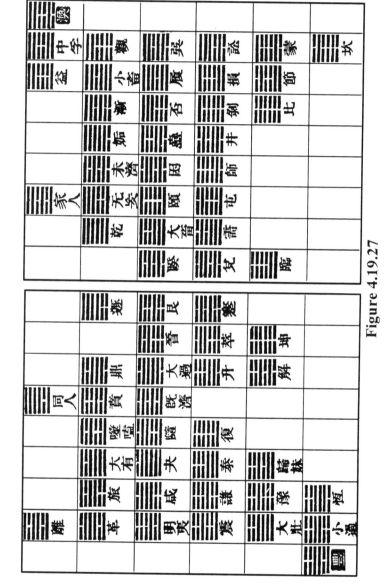

Figure 4.19.27

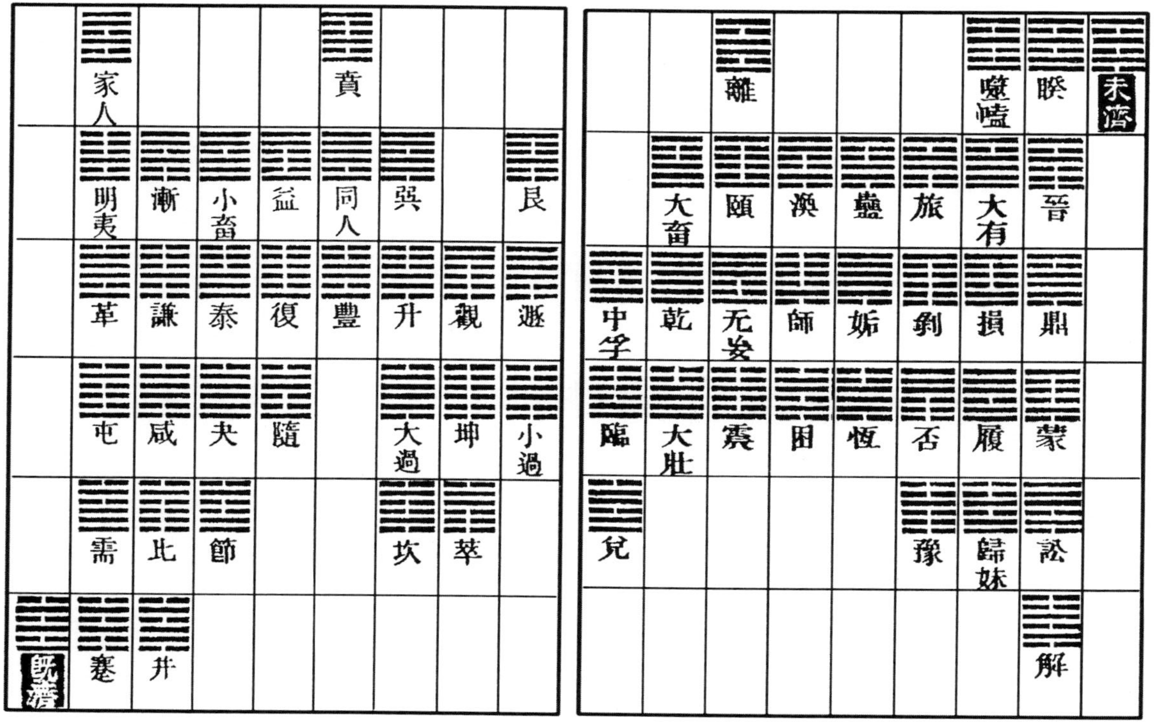

Figure 4.19.28

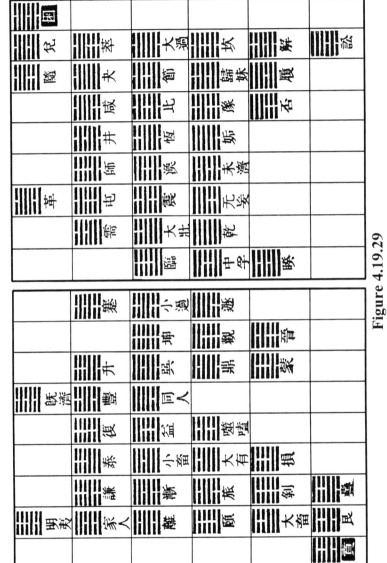

Figure 4.19.29

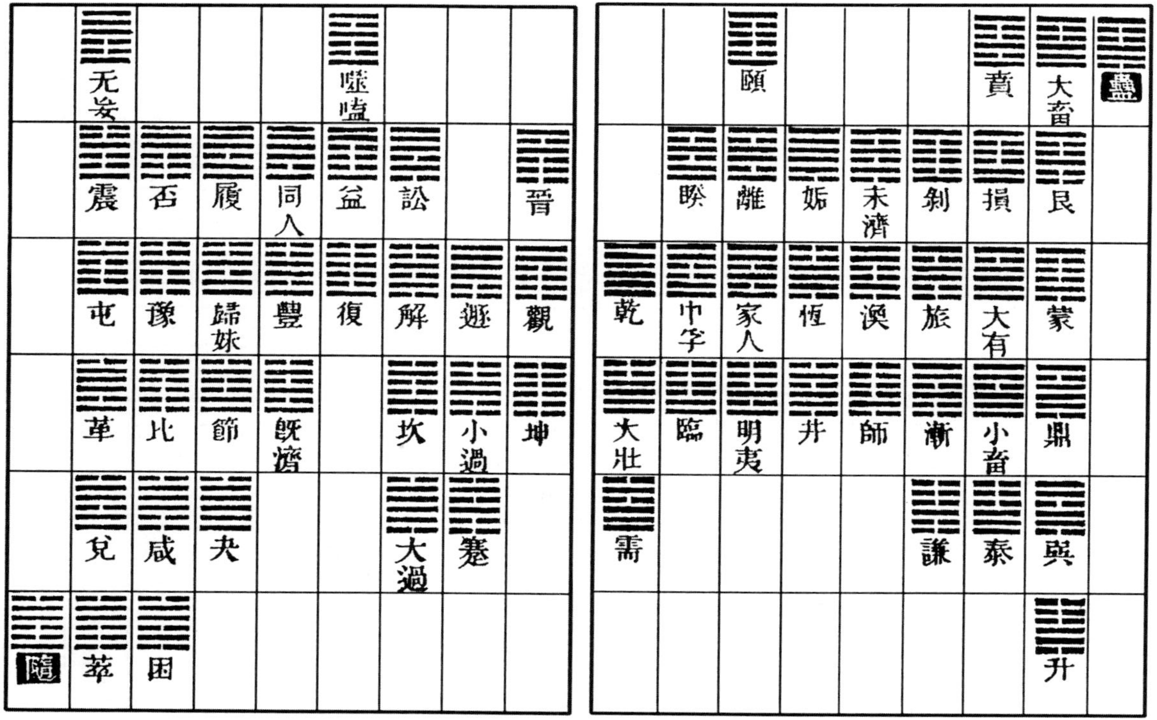

Figure 4.19.30

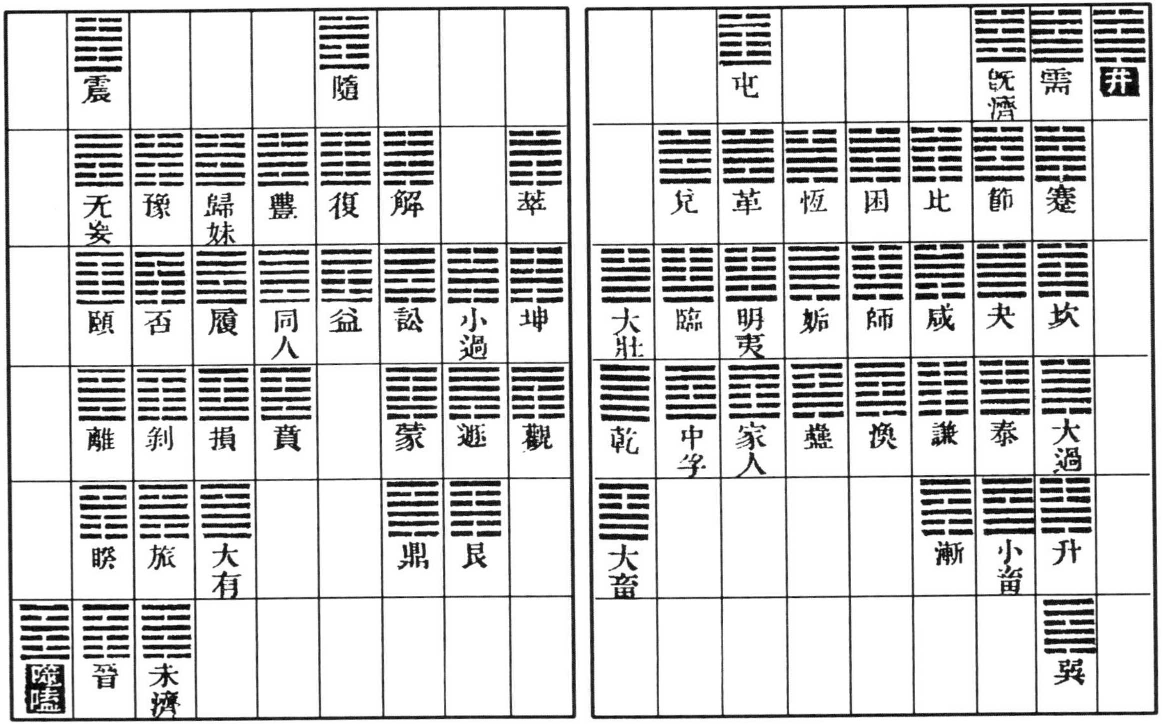

䷖ 剝						
䷄ 需	䷎ 謙	䷜ 坎	䷛ 大過	䷭ 升	䷸ 巽	
䷾ 既濟	䷻ 節	䷪ 夬	䷊ 泰	䷈ 小畜		
	䷇ 比	䷞ 咸	䷎ 謙	䷴ 漸		
	䷮ 困	䷆ 師	䷠ 遯			
	䷟ 恆	䷫ 姤	䷑ 蠱			
䷂ 屯	䷰ 革	䷣ 明夷	䷤ 家人			
	䷹ 兌	䷒ 臨	䷼ 中孚			
		�大壯	䷀ 乾	䷙ 大畜		

	䷬ 萃	䷁ 坤	䷓ 觀			
		䷽ 小過	䷠ 遯	䷳ 艮		
	䷧ 解	䷅ 訟	䷃ 蒙	䷱ 鼎		
䷐ 隨	䷗ 復	䷩ 益				
	䷶ 豐	䷌ 同人	䷕ 賁			
	䷵ 歸妹	䷉ 履	䷨ 損	䷍ 大有		
	䷏ 豫	䷋ 否	䷖ 剝	䷷ 旅	䷿ 未濟	
䷲ 震	䷘ 无妄	䷚ 頤	䷝ 離	䷥ 睽	䷢ 晉	
						䷔ 噬嗑

Figure 4.19.31

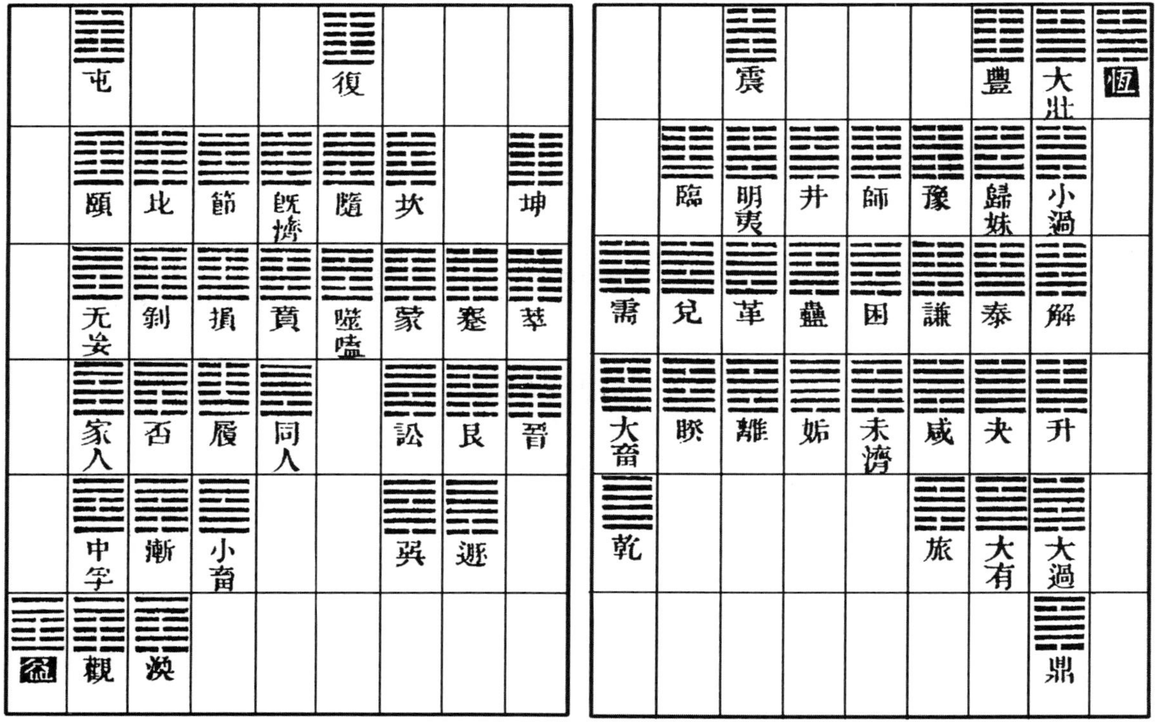

Figure 4.19.32

Notes

[1] Chu Hsi is referring here to the myth of Fu-hsi's creation of the *I* found in the *Hsi-tz'u* (Appended Remarks) appendix to the *I Ching* (section B.2), which he quotes at the beginning of chapter 2 (below).

[2] These are some of the formulaic responses that probably constitute one of the earliest textual layers of the *I Ching*.

[3] I.e. the inherent dynamism of the hexagram system describes a continuous process of change.

[4] I.e., it was not; it was a manifestation of "natural principle," (*tzu-jan chih li*), or the natural order of things.

[5] I.e., the *i-li* school of interpretation.

[6] The *hsiang-shu* school.

[7] Referring to correlative thought, such as the Five Phases theory.

[8] Ts'ai Yüan-ting (or Ts'ai Chi-t'ung, 1135-1198) was a friend and follower of Chu Hsi who was an expert on such esoterica as the symbolism of the pitch-pipes. See Huang Tsung-hsi, *Sung-Yüan hsüeh-an* (A Scholarly Record of the Sung and Yüan Dynasties) (Ssu-pu pei-yao ed.), ch. 62, and Wing-tsit Chan, *Chu Tzu men-jen* (Chu Hsi's Disciples) (Taipei: Student Bookstore, 1982), pp. 331-332. Some scholars (e.g. Mao Huaixin, in Wing-tsit Chan, ed., *Chu Hsi and Neo-Confucianism* [Honolulu: University of Hawaii Press, 1986], p. 508) think that the *I-hsüeh ch'i-meng* was originally drafted by Ts'ai, but a close reading of the text suggests that Chu first drafted it and then sent it to Ts'ai for comments and additions. Chu comments on something written by Ts'ai only once (at the end of chapter III), while Ts'ai's comments on Chu's text are much

more numerous. In any case, Ts'ai is never listed as an author. His portions of the text, in the Chinese, are printed in smaller typeface, in single columns (although in the *Chou-i che-chung* edition the difference is almost too slight to be noticeable). They thus can be considered "notes" to Chu Hsi's text. In this translation Ts'ai's sections are indented. In only two cases does the text explicitly say "Ts'ai Yüan-ting says," but to all others I have added his name in brackets.

[9] This refers to the passages from the *Classic* itself, which are distinguished here by boldface type. In the Chinese text they are the sections that extend to the top of the columns.

[10] At this time Chu Hsi had the bureaucratic post of superintendent of Yün-t'ai (Cloud Terrace) Temple, in Shen-hsi. See Wing-tsit Chan, *Chu Hsi: New Studies* (Honolulu: University of Hawaii Press, 1989), p. 33. Li Kuang-ti, the editor and compiler of the *Chou-i che-chung*, omits all of this sentence except the date (p. 1204).

[11] *Ping-wu* is the number of the year in the 60-year calendrical cycle, which is counted with ten "stems" in combination with twelve "branches." Ch'un-hsi is the name of the last of three reign-periods of Emperor Hsiao-tsung of the Sung (r. 1163-1189).

[12] The *Ho-t'u* ([Yellow] River Chart) and *Lo-shu* (Lo [River] Text) occupy a prominent place in the lore of the *I Ching*, although their connection with the Classic is based on myth and numerology (number symbolism). Note that the *Lo-shu* is a "magic square," in which the sum of three adjacent numbers in any direction is 15. Since Chu Hsi believed that the appendices of the *I Ching* were written by Confucius and were historically reliable, the fact that these charts are mentioned there, and are attested by other writers whom he regarded as reliable, meant that their numerological patterns were a meaningful reflection of the moral/natural order. He saw it as part of the responsibility of a teacher of *Tao-hsüeh*, the Learning of the Way, to demonstrate this internal coherence. The

classic Ch'ing dynasty (1644-1911) refutation of the historical authenticity of these and other diagrams associated with the *I Ching* is Hu Wei, *I-t'u ming-p'ien* (Clarification of the Charts of the *I*) (rpt. Taipei: Kuang-wen Book Co., 1971). See also Joseph Needham's discussion of the *Ho-t'u* and *Lo-shu* in *Science and Civilisation in China*, vol. 3 (Cambridge: Cambridge University Press, 1959), pp. 55-62.

[13]*Ta-chuan,* another name for the *Hsi-tz'u* (Appended Remarks) appendix of the *I Ching*.

[14]*I Ching* (Classic of Changes), *Hsi-tz'u* (Appended Remarks), A.11.8. Chu Hsi, *Chou-i pen-i* (Original Meaning of the *Classic of Change*) (1177; rpt. Taipei: Hua-lien, 1978). "The River" refers to the Yellow River, or Huang-ho. The Lo River (Lo-shui) is a tributary of it in Honan province. Whether the text means "Sage" or "Sages" is debatable. Chu Hsi interprets it in the singular (see his comment below, p. 5), although the traditionally accepted account is the one given below, involving two mythic sages.

[15]Yü is the mythic sage-king who controlled the flooding of the Yellow River by building dikes and levees, and arranged the known world into nine divisions. He is also known as the founder of the first dynasty, the Hsia, which is not historically documented. The classic accounts of Yü are contained in the *Shu Ching*, or Classic of Documents. See James Legge, trans., *The Chinese Classics*, vol. 3, *The Shoo King*, 2nd ed. (1893; rpt. Hong Kong: Hong Kong University Press, 1960), pp. 52-67.

[16]Liu Hsin (d. 23 CE) and his father, Liu Hsiang, were official librarians of the Former Han dynasty (206 BCE - 9 CE).

[17]Warp/woof (*ching/wei*) and outside/inside (*piao/li*) are both standard ways of expressing a complementary relationship.

[18]Kuan Tzu-ming, or Kuan Lang (5th c. CE), wrote a commentary on the *I* from a *hsiang-shu* perspective.

[19] Shao Yung (1011-1077) is considered one of the founders of the Neo-Confucian movement, although he was a somewhat marginal figure. He was a friend of the Ch'eng brothers, and was known primarily as a numerologist and divination expert. He promoted the *Hsien-t'ien* (Before Heaven, or *A priori*) sequence of the hexagrams, associated with Fu-hsi.

[20] *Huang-chi ching-shih shu* (Book of Supreme Principles for Governing the World) (Ssu-pu pei-yao ed.), 7B:10a.. "The circle" refers to the *Ho-t'u*.

[21] The calendrical records and methods are those of the experts who calculated the calendar for each dynasty. The "tones" refers to the correlative theory by which the Five Tones, or musical pitches, were related to the Five Phases, and thus to everything else in the Five Phases system of correlations, including periods of time. (The Five Phases – often misleadingly translated as "Five Elements" – are earth, wood, metal, fire, and water.) The intercalary period is that which needs to be added to make the lunar year correspond to the solar year.

[22] *Huang-chi ching-shih shu* 7B.10a. "The square" refers to the *Lo-shu*. The well-field system, which was thought to be have been used at the beginning of the Chou dynasty, divides plots of land into 3x3 grids of nine squares. The eight outer squares are each tilled and the produce kept by one family, while the central, inner square is tilled jointly with the produce given as tax to the central government. Mencius looked back favorably on this idealized system (there is no evidence that it was ever actually practiced), as did Chang Tsai, one of the 11th-century founders of Neo-Confucianism.

[23] One *mu* is about 1/6 of an acre.

[24] Both Fu-hsi and King Wen are mentioned here because circular arrangements of the trigrams are associated with each of them (see below, Chapter II, Figures 10 and 12).

[24] Both Fu-hsi and King Wen are mentioned here because circular arrangements of the trigrams are associated with each of them (see below, Chapter II, Figures 10 and 12).

[25] Viscount Chi is the narrator of the "Great Plan" (*Hung-fan*) chapter of the *Shu-ching* (Classic of Documents), which describes the nine-point plan for ordering the world that was given by Heaven to Yü. See James Legge, *The Shoo King*, pp. 320-344; and Wing-tsit Chan, *Source Book*, pp. 8-11.

[26] *Huang-chi ching-shih shu* 7B:10a.

[27] Pan Ku (d. 92 CE) was an official historian of the Former Han dynasty. Ch'en T'uan was a 10th-century Taoist priest who, it is traditionally thought, may have been the source of several diagrams related to the *I Ching* that eventually were incorporated into the Sung Neo-Confucian synthesis. These include, in addition to the *Ho-t'u* and *Lo-shu*, Shao Yung's *Hsien-t'ien* (Before Heaven) diagram and Chou Tun-i's *T'ai-chi* (Supreme Polarity) diagram. Liu Mu (1011-1064) was one of the links in the transmission.

The typeface indicates that Ts'ai Yüan-ting's comment continues at this point all the way to the next quote from the *I Ching* ("Heaven is one"). However, there appears to be a shift in voice at this point. Ts'ai was the expert on such topics as numerology and the lore of the various diagrams, and his portions of the text consistently stick to straightforward explanation of these details. But here we see a clear shift to issues of a more general, philosophical order – and specifically to the idea of the unity of natural principle (*tzu-jan chih li*), a favorite topic of Chu Hsi's. I am therefore quite confident that what follows is Chu Hsi's voice.

[28] In other words, Chu Hsi is interpreting *sheng-jen* (in the *Hsi-tz'u* passage quote above) in the singular, meaning "the Sage" (Fu-hsi), rather than "the Sages" (Fu-hsi and Yü) – despite the contrary interpretation by the majority of former scholars.

[30] See the alternative version of the creation of the *I*, which Chu Hsi prefers, in section 2 below.

[31] The total is 60, not 120, because of the way the sequence proceeds. Instead of matching each of the 12 branches with the first stem, then again with the second and so on, the order is: s1-b1, s2-b2, ... s10-b10, s1-b11, s2-b12, s3-b1, etc. This procedure comes back to s1-b1 after 60.

[32] Chu Hsi is referring here to Taoist concepts that were marginally acceptable to him. "Circulating *ch'i*" refers to Taoist meditation; "Kinship of the Three" refers to a Taoist alchemical text (*Ts'an-t'ung ch'i*) on which Chu wrote a commentary; and the Supreme One was a Taoist divinity, associated in Taoism with *T'ai-chi* (Supreme Polarity), a term that was borrowed by Chou Tun-i and was crucial to Chu Hsi's philosophical synthesis.

[33] Paraphrasing the story quoted at the beginning of chapter 2 below (*Hsi-tz'u* B.2.1).

[34] *Hsi-tz'u* A.11.8.

[35] *Hsi-tz'u* A.10.1.

[36] *Hsi-tz'u* A.11.7.

[37] *Hsi-tz'u* A.9.1.

[38] In traditional Chinese cartography, North is at the bottom.

[39] That is, numbers are logically derived from the principle of bipolarity, and in the *Ho-t'u* the numbers 1 through 10 are arrayed in five groups, each with a *yin* (even) and *yang* (odd) number.

[40] *Shuo-kua* ("Explanating the Trigrams" appendix of the *Classic of Change*), 1. In other words, in order to make the line from the *shuo-kua* correspond to the *Ho-t'u* and *Lo-shu*, Chu Hsi blithely

[40] *Shuo-kua* ("Exploring the Trigrams" appendix of the *Classic of Change*), 1. In other words, in order to make the line from the *shu-kua* correspond to the *Ho-t'u* and *Lo-shu*, Chu Hsi blithely introduces the fudge factor of "taking 2 as 1" in the case of the square, and approximating *pi* as 3 in the case of the circle.

[41] That is, the evens = 30 and the odds = 25.

[42] That is, by deleting the central 5 of the River Chart and the central 5 and 10 of the Lo Text, both diagrams contain the numbers 1, 2, 3, 4, 6, 7, 8, and 9. Of these, the sums of both the odd numbers (*yang*) and the even numbers (*yin*) are 20.

[43] This and the next paragraph refer to various sequences of the Five Phases associated with the Yin-yang or "Naturalist" school of thought, founded by Tsou Yen (4th-3rd c. BCE). (See Joseph Needham, *Science and Civilisation in China*, vol. 2 (Cambridge: Cambridge University Press, 1956), pp. 253-261.) The sequences are obtained here by substituting for each number of the diagram the Phase correlated with it, according to Chu Hsi's commentary above (p. 7).

[44] This is traditionally called the "mutual production" (*hsiang-sheng*) sequence. The logic is that wood produces fire (when burned), which produces earth (ash), which produces metal (ores), which produces water (or liquid, when melted), which returns to produce wood (or vegetation).

[45] This is the "mutual conquest" sequence: water quenches fire, which melts metal, which cuts wood, which blocks or contains earth (in the ancient "rammed earth" method of building walls), which blocks water (in dams and dikes).

[46] These are the numbers that yield the solid and broken lines of the hexagrams in the method of divination: the even numbers are *yin*

⁴⁷I.e., eliminating the central 5 and 10 from the ten numbers of the River Chart yielded the eight trigrams. I am not sure what the second sentence means; the sum of Lo Text numbers is 45, which has no particular significance in the *I ching*.

⁴⁸"Supreme Polarity," "Two Modes," and "Four Images" are terms from *His-tz'u* A.11.5, quoted at the beginning of the next chapter (p. 15). See note 53 for an explanation of the terms.

⁴⁹These categories all come from the *Hung-fan* (Great Plan) chapter of the *Shu Ching* (Classic of Documents).

⁵⁰See *Hsi-tz'u* A.9.3 (quoted below at the beginning of chapter III), which is the earliest extant usage of the term "Great Amplification" (*ta-yen*). Commentators have various ways of deriving this number (see Lynn, *Classic of Changes*, p. 73, n.36).

⁵¹In this chapter Chu Hsi proceeds to the core of the *I Ching*, the trigrams and hexagrams, to explain the *yin-yang* theory and symbolism that the *I* represented. *Yin-yang* theory is quite central to his entire system, as it constitutes the simplest and most fundamental form of order, or principle (*li*).

⁵²*Hsi-tz'u* B.2.1. This passage is the premise for Chu Hsi's entire approach to the *I Ching*.

⁵³*Hsi-tz'u* A.11.5. *T'ai-chi*, which is usually translated as "Supreme Ultimate," in Chu Hsi's interpretation means the fundamental ordering principle (*li*) of the cosmos, which is the principle of *yin-yang* polarity. The "Two Modes" are *yin* and *yang*, each divided into young and mature phases. When they each subdivide further they yield the Eight Trigrams.

⁵⁴ See Ch'eng Hui, *Chou-I ku chan-fa* (Ancient methods of *I-ching* divination, 1160) in *Fan-shih erh-shih-I chung ch'I-shu* (Pai-pu ts'ung-shu chi-ch'eng ed.), v. 5, p. 1a (an anecdote about Ch'eng Hao and Shao Yung).

⁵⁴ See Ch'eng Hui, *Chou-I ku chan-fa* (Ancient methods of *I-ching* divination, 1160) in *Fan-shih erh-shih-i chung ch'i-shu* (Pai-pu ts'ung-shu chi-ch'eng ed.), v. 5, p. 1a (an anecdote about Ch'eng Hao and Shao Yung).

⁵⁵See Chou Tun-i, *T'ai-chi-t'u shuo* (Explanation of the Supreme Polarity Diagram), in Wm. Theodore de Bary and Irene Bloom, eds., *Sources of Chinese Tradition*, 2nd ed. (New York: Columbia University Press, 1999), vol. 1, pp. 672-676.

⁵⁶ "*Ho-t'u t'ien-ti ch'üan-shu*" (The complete numbers of Heaven and Earth in the River Chart), in *Huang-chi ching-shih shu*, 7A.23a.

⁵⁷ "*Hsin-hsüeh*" (The study of the mind), in *Huang-chi ching-shih shu*, 8B.25a.

⁵⁸Chou Tun-i, *T'ai-chi-t'u shuo*.

⁵⁹Shao Yung, *Huang-chi ching-shih shu*, 7A:24b (see below for the whole passage). Cf. also Shao Yung (or his son Shao Po-wen), *Yü-ch'iao wen-tui* (Dialogue of the Fisherman and the Woodcutter), in sec. 10: "One and Two are the Two Modes."

⁶⁰*T'ai-chi-t'u shuo*, leaving out earth. Chou's statement is, "The alternation and combination of *yang* and *yin* generate water, fire, wood, metal, and earth."

⁶¹*Huang-chi ching-shih shu*, 7A:24b (below, p. 22).

⁶² *San-tsai*, referring to Heaven, Mankind, and Earth. At this level of differentiation the diagrams begin to reflect the structure of the cosmos.

⁶³*Chou-li* (Rituals of Chou), ch. 24, "Ta-pu" (Great Divination) section, referring to three different divination texts: The *Lien-shan*, *Kuei-tsang*, and *Chou-i*, corresponding to the three ancient dynasties, Hsia, Shang, and Chou. The *Lien-shan* and *Kuei-tsang* have never

[65] *Huang-chi ching-shih shu*, 7A:24b.

[66] Ibid.

[67] Ibid.

[68] *Chou-li*, loc. cit.

[69] *Hsi-tz'u* B.1.1.

[70] *Huang-chi ching-shih shu*, 7A:24b.

[71] Chiao Kan (Yen-shou) lived in the 1st century BCE and was one of the earliest representatives of the *hsiang-shu* school of interpretation, along with Meng Hsi and Ching Fang. In his book (*Chiao-shih I-lin* [Mr. Chiao's Grove of Changes], Ssu-pu pei-yao ed.) he pairs each of the hexagrams with each of the others, resulting in 4,096 pairs, to each of which he attaches a text.

[72] This enigmatic passage is explained in the comments and notes below. besides a possible reference to one of the circular arrangements of trigrams (see below), the general idea seems to be that knowing the past is natural, while the capacity to divine the future is part of the oracle's "spiritual" nature (see *Hsi-tz'u*).

[73] *I Ching, Shuo-kua* (Explaining the Trigrams) appendix, 4.

[74] This undoubtedly refers to one of two common Chinese cosmological models, called *kai-t'ien* (dome heaven) and *hun-t'ien* (spherical heaven). In the former, heaven and earth are like nested hemispherical domes; in the latter they are like concentric spheres. In both models heaven rotates counter-clockwise around the earth. The heavenly bodies move clockwise in relation to heaven, but more slowly than heaven's rotation, so they appear to move counter-clockwise (east to west). See Joseph Needham, *Science and Civilisation in China*, vol. 3, pp. 210-219.

In both models heaven rotates counter-clockwise around the earth. The heavenly bodies move clockwise in relation to heaven, but more slowly than heaven's rotation, so they appear to move counter-clockwise (east to west). See Joseph Needham, *Science and Civilisation in China*, vol. 3, pp. 210-219.

Shao Yung here is, in effect, superimposing this counterclockwise rotation of heaven onto the circular sequence of Fu-hsi's chart, in which the temporal sequence of the seasons associated with the trigrams is clockwise. Thus to move from the present to the future, as in divination, one is moving clockwise, which is opposite to the rotation of heaven. To put it another way, while the seasons progress clockwise on the Fu-hsi chart – summer, fall, winter, spring – from the fixed human perspective the present becomes the past. Since the *I Ching* provides a method, through its numbers, of seeing from the present to the future, it is opposite to the natural flow. Hence "the *I* has reverse calculations."

The difficulty with this rationale is that it does not really involve the numbers assigned to the trigrams, which do not entirely fit the model – only on the right side of the circular chart (Fig. 10) does the sequence of numbers correspond to the progress of seasons (as Ts'ai Yüan-ting acknowledges below). This gives *I Ching* commentators a great deal of trouble; every one seems to have a different way of explaining it, ranging from simple avoidance to rather ingenious methods.

The problem may in fact be a spurious one. In the Mawangdui manuscript of the *I Ching*, discovered in 1973, the corresponding line reads, "The *I* has *penetrating* numbers." The character for "penetrating" (*ta*) could easily have been mistaken for *ni* "reverse" by a careless copyist – if the manuscript actually predates the "received" version of the text. This is not certain, despite the fact that the Mawangdui manuscript dates from about 190 B.C.E. and the received version is the one embedded in the commentary by

[75] *Huang-chi ching-shih shu,* 7A:24a.

[76] The *Chou-i che-chung* edition of the *I-hsüeh ch'i-meng* contains the following note at this point (p. 1254):

> Master *Chu's Classified Conversations* (*Chu Tzu yü-lei*) says: "If we start from Ch'ien in the first position and arrange horizontally to K'un in the eighth, this is completely natural. Therefore the *Shuo-kua* says, 'The *Changes* consists in backwards-moving numbers.' It is always from the already arisen hexagrams that the not yet arisen hexagrams are attained. Supposing we take the circular chart it should be like this; only then do we see the decline and growth of *yin* and *yang* in successive stages: Chen has one *yang*, Li and Tui have two *yang*, and Ch'ien has three *yang*. Sun has one *yin*, K'an and Ken have two *yin*, and K'un has three *yin*. Although this appears to be a somewhat facile arrangement, it is nevertheless nothing but natural principle."

In other words, according to Chu, it may be contrary in the sense mentioned above, but there is still a rational basis for it.

[77] *Huang-chi ching-shih shu,* 7A:24b.

[78] *Huang-chi ching-shih shu,* 7A:25b.

[79] Cf. Chou Tun-i's *T'ai-chi-t'u shuo* (Explanation of the Supreme Polarity Diagram), which begins with the enigmatic line, *Wu-chi erh t'ai-chi* ("Non-polar and yet Supreme Polarity!"). The meaning may be that even in an undifferentiated state there is the potential for polarity or differentiation, or, as Shao says, *yin* contains *yang*.

[80] *Huang-chi ching-shih shu,* 7A:25b.

[81] *Huang-chi ching-shih shu,* 7A:26a.

I-hsüeh ch'i-meng

[80] *Huang-chi ching-shih shu*, 7A:25b.

[81] *Huang-chi ching-shih shu*, 7A:26a. The last three sentences rely on the principle that the natural movement of *yang* is upward, and that of *yin* is downward. Thus T'ai is an image of harmonious but dynamic interaction, while P'i symbolizes stability.

[82] *Huang-chi ching-shih shu*, 7A:26b.

[83] *Huang-chi ching-shih shu*, 8A:22a. In Shao's text this is followed by a comment by Huang Yüeh-chou, a Ming dynasty (1368-1644) commentator:

> When onto Ch'ien in the first position are added the Eight Trigrams, there are in all 8 times 6 or 48 lines. The lower trigrams are all Ch'ien, yielding 24 *yang* lines. In the upper trigrams there are 12 *yang*, altogether making 36 *yang* lines. The difference is 12 *yin* lines. Of these four divisions of 12, three divisions [3/4] are *yang* lines, and one division is *yin* lines that have prevailed [over the *yang*]. In K'un there are three-quarters *yin* and one-quarter *yang*, which are the *yang* lines that were subdued and taken from Ch'ien. Therefore Ch'ien gets 36 *yang* and mainly progresses, while K'un gets only 12 *yang* and mainly diminishes. The progress is the 360 days, corresponding to the days in the year. The diminution is the 12 days lacking from the 12-month year, which are added as the intercalary number. Thus, the *yin* of K'un is not only without progress, it also overcomes 12 days of Ch'ien, further diminishing (*Huang-chi ching-shih shu*, 8A.22a).

[84] *Huang-chi ching-shih shu*, 7B:12b. Cf. p. 29 below, where the King Wen sequence is called the "functioning" of the *I*.

[85] *Huang-chi ching-shih shu*, 7A:33b-34a.

[86] *Huang-chi ching-shih shu*, 7A:32b.

to clarify Shao Yung's understanding of the term. For him, the *hsien-t'ien* sequence of the trigrams and hexagrams (see Figs. 10 and 11) reflects the ultimate principle of *yin-yang* bipolarity; it is based on the inherent form of the diagrams and thus is prior to experience. The King Wen sequence, which is also called the *hou-t'ien* or "After Heaven" sequence, reflects the virtues or attributes of the diagrams (as Li Kuang-ti suggests – see final note to this chapter), and thus is derived from their functioning in the world. Or to use Immanuel Kant's terminology, the *hsien-t'ien* sequence is analytic, while the *hou-t'ien* sequence is synthetic, or *a posteriori*. Cf. *Huang-chi ching-shih shu* 7B:13a: "*A priori* studies are mental (*hsin*). *A posteriori* studies are empirical (*chi*, traces)."

[88] *Huang-chi ching-shih shu*, 7A:34b.

[89] *Shuo-kua* 5.

[90] *Shuo-kua* 6.

[91] *Huang-chi ching-shih shu*, 7B:11a.

[92] This paragraph and the next are concerned with the differences between the Fu-hsi sequence (Fig. 10) and the King Wen sequence (Fig. 12).

[93] Quoting *Hsi-tz'u* A.5.1: "The alternation of *yin* and *yang* is what is meant by the Way."

[94] *Huang-chi ching-shih shu*, 7B:11b. "Functioning" here and in the following passages refers to trigrams that are dynamic or changing.

[95] *Huang-chi ching-shih shu*, 7B:12b.

[96] Ibid. Cf. above, p. 25: the Fu-hsi sequence is the "foundation" (*pen*) – equivalent here to the "substance" (*t'i*) of the *I*.

[97] *Shuo-kua* 7.

[98] *Shuo-kua* 8.

I-hsüeh ch'i-meng

---

[97] *Shuo-kua* 7.

[98] *Shuo-kua* 8.

[99] *Hsi-tz'u* B.2.1, quoted at the beginning of this chapter.

[100] *Shuo-kua* 9.

[101] *Hsi-tz'u* B.2.1. Note by Li Kuang-ti in *Chou-i che-chung* (p. 1270):

> In *Master Chu's Classified Conversations* it says: "Fu-hsi drew the Eight Trigrams, but these several drawings completely exhaust the principles of all things in the world. Students who can understand them in words are shallow; those who can understand them in images are profound. Neither Wang Fu-ssu [Wang Pi] nor [Ch'eng] I-ch'uan trusted the images. I-ch'uan, discussing the images, only spoke of them as metaphors. Kuo Tzu-ho [Kuo Yung, 1104-1200] said, 'It is not only these terms Heaven and Earth, Thunder and Wind, Water and Fire, Mountain and Lake that we call images; rather the trigram drawings are precisely the images.' This is well said. Cheng Tung-hsiang [Cheng Hsüan, 127-200] concentrates on the images, for example taking Ting [hex. 50] as a caldron, Ko [hex. 49] as a stove, Hsiao Kuo [hex. 62] as a flying bird. There is good reason for this, but to thoroughly crave this kind of connection and correspondence is simply groundless. Students should first understand the correct and proper Principle of the Way. Only then will they manage to collect these various broken fragments and use them in helpful combinations. This will not be unprofitable."

This is a good example of Chu His's attempt to strike a mean between the *i-li* and *hsiang-shu* approaches (cf. Introduction, pp. vi-vii).

[103] "9 in the first place" means a *yang* line in the first (bottom) position of the hexagram.

[104] In Li Kuang-ti's long comment at the end of this section in the *Chou-i che-chung*, he explains that the *A priori* (Fu-hsi) sequence is arranged according to the images of the trigrams (e.g. Heaven and Earth), with Ch'ien and K'un on the vertical axis, and that it reflects their form and substance. The *a posteriori* (King Wen) sequence is arranged according to the virtues or attributes of the trigrams (e.g. active, penetrating), with Chen and Tui on the vertical axis, and it reflects their nature, disposition, and function.

[105] In this chapter Chu reconstructs the method of milfoil (yarrow-stalk) divination from the fragmentary remains contained in the *Hsi-tz'u* appendix. Whether the method he derives is actually one that was formerly used is open to question. It has, however, become standard to this day. A later and simpler method, using three coins, was already in practice in his day, but he did not regard it as authentic. For a concise summary of Chu His's method, see the appendix to the Wilhelm/Baynes translation of the *I Ching* (3rd ed., pp. 721-724).

[106] *Hsi-tz'u* A.9.3.

[107] I.e., 5 is a prime number and a necessary factor of 50.

[108] Refer to Fig. 1. The 7 and 2 at the top are 9, which is the number of mature *yang*. The 6 and 2 at the bottom are 7, young *yang*. The totals on the left and right are 11 and 13, which after subtracting 5 are 6 and 8, the numbers of mature and young *yin*.

[109] *His-tz'u* A.9.3.

[110] Note in *Chou-i che-chung*, p. 1276:

> Ts'ui Ching said, "The 49 that are used are modeled after the mature *yang*'s 7 times 7. The 64 hexagrams likewise are

Ts'ui Ching said, "The 49 that are used are modeled after the growing *yang*'s 7 times 7. The 64 hexagrams likewise are modeled after the growing *yin*'s 8 times 8.... 'The milfoil is round and spiritual,' symbolizing Heaven; 'the hexagrams are square and wise,' symbolizing Earth (quoting *Hsi-tz'u* A.11.2). This is the distinction between *yin* and *yang*. The one that is discarded and not used symbolizes the Supreme Polarity."

[111]*Hsi-tz'u* A.9.3.

[112]The *Chou-i che-chung* (p. 1285) contains a comment here by Ts'ai Yüan-ting that is not part of the *I-hsüeh ch'i-meng*, in which he summarizes the line frequencies. Here is a summary of it:

Table 1:

Mature *yang*: 12 +   Young *yang*:   20   =   32 Substance (*t'i*)
Mature *yin*:   4 +   Young *yin*:   28   =   32 Function (*yung*)
                16 +   48   =   64

Mature *yang* and Mature *yin* are the images of Ch'ien and K'un, with frequencies of 2 x 8 = 16. Young *yang* and Young *yin* are the images of the six children, with frequencies of 6 x 8 = 48.

[113]*Hsi-tz'u* A.9.3.

[114]*Hsi-tz'u* A.9.6.

[115]*I-hsing* (682-727) was a Buddhist monk, astronomer, and mathematician who wrote a commentary on the *I Ching*. I have not identified Pi Chung-ho and Ku T'uan. All three are quoted by the T'ang dynasty poet and essayist Liu Yü-hsi (772-842) in his "Discussing the [numbers] Nine and Six in the *I* (*Pien I chiu liu lun*)

[116] That is, starting with 49 stalks instead of 50 would result in a static system in which *yin* and *yang* would not function because their numbers would always be equal.

[117] That is, the Sage's perfect wisdom hit upon exactly the right method to yield an instrument for detecting the dynamic pattern of Change, or the dynamic pattern of "natural principle" (*tzu-jan chih li*).

[118] **Table 2** (translator's summary):

	Mature *yang*	Young *yin*	Young *yang*	Mature *yin*
Counted off:	36	32	28	24
Placed between fingers:	12	16	20	24
	(4+4+4, counted as 3+3+3 = 9,	(-->8)	(-->7)	(8+8+8, counted as 2+2+2 = 6,

[119] This is a basic statement of Chu Hsi's understanding of *t'ai-chi* and *yin-yang*: both the unity and difference are real.

[120] *Huang-chi ching-shih shu*, 7A:7b.

[121] *Hsi-tz'u* A.9.4.

[122] *Hsi-tz'u* A.9.5.

[123] *Hsi-tz'u* A.9.6-8.

[124] Chu Hsi gives no explanation for the use of the word *i* here in the text, instead of the word *pien*, which he consistently uses to mean each of the three "changes" that constitute one line. The text seems to be inconsistent, as in the next clause it uses *pien* to refer to the same thing. The colloquial word for "change" was *pien-i*, which has the connotation of alternating change between phases, such as *yin-yang* alternation.

i, which has the connotation of alternating change between phases, such as *yin-yang* alternation.

[125] These are four of the simple oracular statements that probably constitute the earliest textual layer of the *I ching* (see Introduction, note 2).

[126]*Hsi-tz'u* A.9.9.

[127]In this chapter Chu explains how to derive a second hexagram from the first, representing the potential future outcome, or prognostication.

[128]Hexagram for Ch'ien. "Using 9s" and "using 6s" refers to the Ch'ien and K'un hexagrams, respectively, obtained with all six lines changing (mature). The "Image" (*Hsiang*) is one of the Ten Wings that comments on the symbolism of the component trigrams.

[129]Referring to the *Wen-yen* (Remarks on the Text) appendix, which is a commentary on just the Ch'ien and K'un hexagrams.

[130]Ou-yang Hsiu (1007-1072) was a prominent scholar and official of the Northern Sung dynasty. One of his major theories regarding the *I* was that Confucius could not have written the Ten Wings.

[131]This applies to all the hexagrams. So, for example, a *yin* line in the second place (counting from the bottom) is called "6 in the second place," and a *yang* line in the fourth place is called "9 in the fourth place,", etc.

[132]This is more commonly called the *kua-tz'u*, or hexagram statement. "*T'uan* statement" (*t'uan-tz'u*) should not be confused with the *T'uan* appendix (*T'uan-chuan*).

[133]*Tso-chuan* (Tso's Commentary to the *Spring and Autumn Annals*), Duke Ch'ao, 7th year. See James Legge, trans., *The Chinese Classics*,

I-hsüeh ch'i-meng

---

[135] Ibid., Duke Min, 1st year. Legge, pp. 124, 125.

[136] Ibid., Duke Ch'ao, 29th year. Legge, pp. 729, 731.

[137] Ibid., Duke Hsi, 25th year. Legge, pp. 194, 195.

[138] Ibid., Duke Chuang, 22nd year. Legge, pp. 102, 103.

[139] Ibid., Duke Chao, 12th year. Legge, pp. 637, 640.

[140] Ibid., Duke Hsi, 15th year. Legge, pp. 165, 169.

[141] The ruler (*chu*) is the governing, or dominant, line of the hexagram.

[142] This case is not in the *Tso-chuan*.

[143] This is part of the hexagram statement of Chun.

[144] *Tso chuan*, Duke Hsiang, 9th year. Legge, pp. 437, 439.

[145] Mu Chiang had been confined to the Eastern Palace for having engaged in some court intrigue. The diviner's response to her indicated that she would soon get out, based on the *T'uan* statement of Sui. But she died there.

[146] *Tso chuan*, Duke Ch'ao, 29th year. Legge, pp. 729, 731. This is the line text for the case of "all nines."

[147] The hexagram statement for K'un reads, in part, "It is beneficial to have the steadiness of the mare. When the superior person has somewhere to go, he at first is lost and then finds it."

[148] The Ch'ien hexagram statement reads only, "Originally penetrating; steadiness is beneficial" (*Yüan heng li chen*). (For a discussion of ways of translating this statement, see Shchutskii, *Researches on the I Ching*, pp. 136-144.) The point here is that with

I-hsüeh ch'i-meng

---

[148] The Ch'ien hexagram statement reads only, "Originally penetrating; steadiness is beneficial" (*Yüan heng li chen*). (For a discussion of ways of translating this statement, see Shchutskii, *Researches on the I Ching*, pp. 136-144.) The point here is that with six lines changing, both hexagram statements and their interrelationships should be interpreted as the prognostication. Neither Chu nor Ts'ai Yüan-ting say why the line text for "all nines" or "all sixes" should not be used.

[149] *Hsi-tz'u* A.9.8.

[150] See above, Chapter II, note 71.